Brand It Like Barack!

How Barack Obama sold himself to America
and what you can learn from this.

By
Gary Kaskowitz

First published by Dog Ear Publishing
4010 W. 86th Street, Ste H
Indianapolis, IN 46268
www.dogearpublishing.net

ISBN: 978-160844-531-8

This book is printed on acid-free paper.

Printed in the United States of America

Dedication

For Elyse, Sara, and Eric, and in loving memory of my
parents, Ernest and Shirley. I could not have completed
this project without the inspiration and encouragement
you have all given me over the years.
Thank you!

Table of Contents

Preface

As I write this, Barack Obama has been serving as President of the United States for a little over a year. This book is not written as a commentary upon the man, his office, or his politics. Rather it is a thorough analysis of how he ran his presidential campaign taking him from a relatively unknown junior Senator to ultimate victory. That Obama was able to accomplish this feat in such a short time span (approximately two years) is, to many, simply amazing.

In the course of my teachings and study I have had the pleasure of analyzing many great marketers and what made them successful. There is a great deal of common ground amongst the greats, not the least of which is that they practice (and do it quite well) powerful marketing principles that help them appeal to the emotions of their customers and engender a great deal of loyalty from them.

While many are curious as to how Barack Obama was able to accomplish his victory in such short order, the answers are there for the taking. There really is no magic to what he did, but if you don't know what to look for it may seem like that! Anyone with proper training and guidance in these classic marketing principles can set themselves apart from the crowd.

This book is intended for any small business person or professional who is looking to rise to the top of your field. It also provides a thorough discussion of what Barack Obama and his campaign team did so effectively to win the presidency, from a marketer's perspective. So, if you are looking to raise your own visibility, or just plain curious how Barack Obama did it, then please enjoy this book!

Gary Kaskowitz, March, 2010

Acknowledgements

Writing a book is not the solo act that many would believe. While the ideas for this book had been formulating in my mind for several years, this book would have remained there forever if not for the support of many along the way.

I am grateful to have had the opportunity to discuss the marketing techniques outlined in this book with my students and colleagues at Moravian College. Their questions have helped refine my thinking and allowed me to express my thoughts more clearly. It is said that the best way to learn a subject is to teach it, and I wholeheartedly agree.

I am thankful for the encouragement and support of my friends and family who prompted me for regular updates helping ensure that this book flowed from my head to paper. My love and thanks go to my parents and siblings who always told me that I could complete a project like this and gave me the belief in myself so crucial to success. Thanks also to Barb and Joe for taking the time to review my early chapters and suggesting that I "follow the money" when discussing how politicians and other brands can bury their competition.

Most importantly, I am grateful and thankful for my wife and children. Elyse, my 'reader', who offered so many hours of discussion, reflection, and encouragement. I would never have written this book without your (loving) nudging to get it done. Eric, my 'support staff', who urged me forward while reminding me to enjoy the process. Your questions and discussions of the topics in this book helped me to clarify my points so that they didn't sound so technical. Sara, my 'editor-in-chief', who proofed my manuscript and helped create a structure I could work with to actually finish the project. You are awesome! I really could not have completed this without my team, and for you I am ever grateful.

CHAPTER 1

Introduction

> *"Thank you so much. (APPLAUSE) Thank you very much. (APPLAUSE) Thank you, everybody. To Chairman Dean and my great friend Dick Durbin, and to all my fellow citizens of this great nation; with profound gratitude and great humility, I accept your nomination for presidency of the United States."*[1]
>
> Barack Obama – Democratic Convention, Denver, CO – August 28, 2008

On January 16, 2007, Barack Obama announced to his supporters that he would seek the presidency of the United States. On November 4, 2008 he achieved that dream.

In 2006, who could have predicted the meteoric rise of the Junior Senator from Illinois, relatively unknown outside of his home state, to become the first African American elected President of the United States? Entering a crowded Democratic field against household names like Hillary Clinton and John Edwards, how was Barack Obama able to not only win his party's nomination but go on to dominate the general election?

On the surface, Barack Obama appeared to have had everything going against him. A self-described "tall, skinny kid with big ears and a funny-sounding name," an African American with less than three years of Congressional experience up against the Democratic Party's presumptive nominee and her entrenched political machine, wouldn't seem to have much of a chance for victory.

Yet victory was indeed his. Barack Obama and his campaign team accomplished in under two years what many people cannot do in a lifetime. In two short years, Barack Obama was able to build an audience of adoring, loyal fans who not only voted for him, but donated time and money in unprecedented numbers. The story of Barack Obama is a fascinating one that future generations will surely tell. Like many good stories, it reads almost like a fairy tale and indeed it follows a classic storytelling structure that has been around for over 3000 years. Barack Obama will surely enter the legends of our history, and rightfully so. Great stories become legends not only for the quality of the story, but for the truth and wisdom that the stories contain. The story of Barack Obama will become a classic because of the many lessons it teaches. In fact, the successful rise of Barack Obama is based on the effective use of classic storytelling and branding principles which, with knowledge and practice, can be applied by anyone looking to dominate his or her market.

On the surface, Barack Obama appeared to have everything going against him; yet victory was indeed his.

The meteoric rise of Barack Obama was not only the groundbreaking election of an African American candidate to the highest post in the country, but also an application of basic principles of marketing and branding that anybody can use to propel themselves from obscurity to dominance in their market. What sets apart market leaders from also-rans is the ability of people and organizations to successfully brand themselves in the face of competition and shifting cultural norms that are constantly affecting our world.

Politicians, small business owners, or anyone looking to compete and win on a large scale must possess a great deal of desire and self-confidence. Drive and ambition are obviously necessary components to success. Individuals with great ideas and desires, however, are often relatively unknown within their markets, and have few resources and little name recognition. The natural question arises; are drive and ambition enough to send you to the top of your field? Unfortunately, the answer is usually, "no."

All is not lost though! Sound strategy and implementation of your plan can lead you from obscurity to dominance at an accelerated pace. Applied marketing, branding, and storytelling principles can mean the difference between President and Secretary of State. Employing an effective branding and storytelling strategy can make you a star in your field, creating adoring fans and leaving your competition in the dust.

> **Like Barack Obama, employing an effective branding and storytelling strategy can make you a star in your field, creating adoring fans and leaving your competition in the dust.**

This book will outline the steps that Barack Obama and his campaign successfully conducted to win the presidency. While there has been and will be debate on the politics of Barack Obama, few could argue about the stunning success of his presidential campaign. Strategically using available assets combined with contextual cues allowed him to understand the needs of his market (the voters) while creating a persona that inspired and motivated his customers to not only vote for him, but to aggressively market him themselves. Inspiring fierce loyalty from his constituents, Obama successfully was able to have his message spread at internet speed to come from seemingly nowhere to win his party's presidential nomination and ultimately the general election.

Barack Obama was successful because he and his team thought and acted like modern marketers. They successfully understood and followed classic and new branding principles such as:

- Understanding your environment to make the best possible strategic choices;

- Powerful branding to set yourself apart from your competition, catapulting yourself from unknown to top of the game;

- Time-proven copywriting and advertising principles to cut through the clutter and make your audience want to take action;

- Harnessing symbolic meaning and metaphor to capture the hearts of your audience;

- Finding and using cultural myths to identify disenfranchised consumers that only you can help, thereby ensuring their unwavering loyalty and support;

- Recognizing natural conflicts in your audience and using these to tell a story that resonate them to action;

- Thoroughly understanding the context within which you are selling and using this knowledge appropriately;

- Finding your voice to create your attractive character making you the ONLY logical choice for your audience to do business with;

- Using proven 3000 year-old story telling structure that your audience is "hard-wired" to understand and respond to;

- Identifying the anxieties of your audience and becoming the market maven to them, thereby making all other solutions mere subsets of your solution;

- Creating congruent and consistent messages that reinforce your brand and further make you the only logical choice of your audience;

- Creating a community of believers and cheerleaders who will not only want to do business with you, but will advocate and sell you in order to be part of your story;

- Spread your message at internet speed and effectively use social media to overcome the resistance of your competition and dominate your market.

Barack Obama won the presidency of the United States because he successfully used these and other principles discussed in this book. **If you're looking to establish a name for yourself in whatever you do, then read this book and learn how to Brand It Like Barack.**

CHAPTER 2

The Power of Branding

"We're running against the most established brand in the Democratic Party for the last two decades."

Barack Obama, Oct. 27, 2007 referring to Hillary Clinton[2]

Consider this a fairy tale for our times. The handsome, young, and benevolent king has been newly coronated. He will rule his kingdom with equal parts love, determination, and fortitude. His subjects loved him to the point where they overwhelmingly declared "Be our King!" thus providing him the mandate to seek better times after the reign of the despot.

Yet this beloved king was not always a beloved king, or even a handsome prince for that matter. Yes, many did consider him handsome, but there were others who found his looks to be an obstacle. As for that prince part, well, let's just say that our hero sprang from more than humble origins. Never really knowing his father, our future king sought meaning for his life through travel of the mind and body. Along his journeys, he encountered the down-trodden and sought to be their voice against the lords of the kingdom who sought to oppress these loyal subjects. Someone had to speak on their behalf! Someone had to fight! Someone needed to roust the despot and rule the kingdom with maturity and strength.

This ambition did not belong to our hero alone though. While his cause was just and right, he faced many obstacles and dragons along the way. For, as would be expected, many others also sought to rule this kingdom. Unluckily for our hero, these others were princes and princesses who had every expectation of one day ruling. They had lands and titles, resources beyond compare. They could crush any upstart interloper with the audacity to challenge them. Our hero, born a mere country boy, what chance did he have?

Refusing to take no for an answer, our hero went straight to the people. He would talk and listen to whoever was willing, whether it was 2, 20, or 20,000. While the princes and princesses ignored him, he discovered the secret of the people! With this secret, the people would take control and he would be their messenger. Newly discovered secret in hand, our hero shared his message far and wide. The people loved him! Rulers of foreign lands sought his council. Supporters of high and low rank came to his aid. Our hero was beyond compare for he, and he alone, had the secret of the people.

Soon, the princes and princesses who opposed him realized the error of their ways. They knew that they could not stand in his way any longer and rather, supported him. Now our hero only had one old dragon left to slay on his way to the castle. The dragon had served the house of the lords for many years and knew a thing or two about battles. Our hero and the dragon met on the field of battle. While the dragon roared, our hero danced nimbly about it. The dragon would roar its fire and our hero would block with his shield while thrusting with his sword. The sword of the Secret! The duel lasted hours, days, and weeks. Eventually, the tired dragon could no longer keep up with our dashing young hero and with the strength of the people in his arm; our hero dispatched the dragon and claimed the keys to the castle.

Yes indeed, a fairy tale for our times. And like any good fairy tale, it is not true.

Economics. The dismal science. While many people would like to ignore economic reality, we all know that this is not possible. The laws of supply and demand do hold. When many people are offering the same product or service, the market will drive the price. If you are seen as interchangeable with your competition, then the market will pick the lowest priced offering available that they are aware of. This simple reality is true whether we are in the business of selling products and services to our market or whether we are individuals or politicians selling ourselves for jobs and elections.

Bottom line: all else being equal, people will "purchase" what they are aware of at the lowest price possible. If you are competing against somebody else and are seen as offering the same thing as they are, you customer will typically decide based on lowest price and availability. After all, why pay more or take on an unknown if you don't need to? Why buy "Tom's Cola" if you can get the original established brand for the same money? Why vote for a "Barack Obama" when you already know a "Hillary Clinton?"

Bottom Line: All else being equal, people will 'purchase' what they are aware of at the lowest price possible.

The Importance of an Identity

In the world of marketing, nothing is worse than not having an identity. If you don't stand out in the mind of your market, then your market will surely not care. If you don't promise unique value to your audience, they will tune you out as quickly as they change TV channels when a boring commercial comes on. And, if your market has never heard of you and don't see a reason to do business with you, then you might as well pack up your bags and go home because, frankly, the party's over.

Yes indeed, nothing is worse than not having an identity. Identity defines who we are and what we do. Identification is crucial to understand when establishing a brand. Without the ability to differentiate one product or service from the next, the mass market will never be able to tell you apart from your competition. Essentially, you become nothing more than an interchangeable commodity. When all products serve the same purpose the consumer will merely look for the one available at the cheapest price when they need it. Unless marketers are able to disrupt this natural tendency, people will default to simple rules of thumb when choosing among offerings. Stereotypes prevail and your audience will opt for the solution that requires the least amount of effort to make.

In the world of politics, this is especially rampant. Many people choose their candidates the same way they choose their laundry detergent; out of habit.[3] Unless the voter has reason to take notice of you, they are most likely to go with the established candidate. There's a very good reason that incumbents usually win elections; the voters know who they are. The same is true in business; unless your audience has reason to seriously consider whatever it is you're offering, they will most likely choose the option that they are more familiar with. Branding allows you to create an identity for yourself or your product.

If your market has never heard of you and don't see a reason to do business with you, then you might as well pack up your bags and go home because, frankly, the party's over.

In simple terms, a brand is nothing more than a way for you to identify yourself and/or your products to your market. It is mental shorthand that consumers use when buying things. When implemented correctly, your brand can add a great deal of value to your business and your bottom line. When branding is done improperly, it can consume resources better spent on other endeavors and actually harm your business.

First we must start with a simple fact; people have either heard of you, or they haven't. If your audience doesn't know you or what you do, then your branding problem is quite simple; you need awareness of your brand. This problem is especially compounded when you are running against an established brand. When Barack Obama entered the primary race against Hillary Clinton, John Edwards, Joe Biden and others he was a relative unknown nationally. At the time of Obama's entry, 37% of the nation's public did not even know who he was. Among likely Democratic voters, less than 10% thought of him as a viable candidate.[4] Yet, he quickly overcame this deficit to become the biggest money magnet the Democratic Party had seen, raising $58 million the first six months of 2007.[5] This was the most cash ever raised by a candidate in a 6-month period in a non-election year. How did Obama do this? By understanding the power of branding.

The Power of Branding

A good brand serves three basic functions: 1) it identifies you in the marketplace; 2) it differentiates you from your competition; 3) it shows a unique promise of value to your audience.

Identification and differentiation of branding are a given, and unfortunately, this is where many politicians and business owners stop. While identification and differentiation are inherent in branding, the best marketers know that powerful brands actually promise unique value to our audience. Slapping the sign "John's Hardware" on your store will identify you and differentiate you from "Sally's Hardware" next door, but it doesn't give people a reason to choose you. Obviously, this begs the question of what is value and how can brands show this.

For many years, marketers were content with merely distinguishing themselves from their competition through mind-share branding.[6] Mind-share branding essentially attempts to own the associations that your audience makes with your product class and your product. If you sell furniture, mind-share branding would suggest that every time a person thinks of a couch, they think of you.[7] Marketers accomplish mind-share branding through a constant repetition of their message with the associations they want to get across. The problem with mind-share branding is that it takes an incredible amount of resources to successfully work. And, for most people resources mean money.

It is true that if you are conducting a mind-share branding campaign, then the person with the bigger war chest will typically prevail. If you are a local hardware store looking to take on Walmart in low pricing, well, good luck. Sorry to say but if your audience is thinking of where to buy cheap light bulbs and it comes down to you and Sam, you'll most likely lose. The same holds true in politics. Whoever amasses more money will usually win. Incumbents in office have been shown to raise almost ten times as much money as challengers, due in large part to the name (i.e., brand) recognition that they already have.[8] At the end of the day, if you are doing mind-share branding, it takes a lot of money to win an election (or to gain market share in business).

> **At the end of the day, if you are doing mind-share branding it takes a lot of money to win an election (or to gain market share in business).**

In essence, with mind-share branding, you want to crowd out all competitive messaging with your own so that your audience selects you out of habit.[9] Constant (and expensive) advertising allows you to be at the forefront of your audiences' thoughts when they think about the product you offer. Obviously, mind-share marketing can be very expensive and beyond the range of most individuals and small-business owners. **The saying "follow the money" is especially true with mind-share branding. If you are going to engage your competition through mind-share branding, you can most likely follow the money to the victor.**

The problems don't stop there though. Mind-share marketing assumes your audience is making what marketers call a low-involvement decision. These decision types are ones that people make without much thought or alternative evaluation. The marketer can't really think of a real difference between his/her product and the competition, and assumes that the audience won't either. We are saying 'beer is beer; fast food is fast food; politicians are politicians. Since all brands are essentially the same and most consumers won't spend too much time thinking about the differences, I want my brand to be at the top of their mind when they do think about whatever I'm selling.' While this strategy can be very successful when people are not emotionally invested in the decision, it can backfire when they are, which is usually in the earlier stages of an election.

Capturing minds takes money

While Barack Obama absolutely did use repetitive advertising and overwhelming messaging later in his campaign, this was not his initial strategy. Once Obama won his party's nomination he essentially conducted mind-share branding in the general election. By this time he had already captured the hearts of his supporters and key opinion leaders and was able to successfully bury John McCain by outspending him in advertising and messaging. Obama successfully raised more than $575 million over the course of his campaign. In the final months of the general election, Obama raised $428 million to McCain's $190 million. In addition, McCain had accepted federal funding thus limiting his spending to $84 million.[10] This amount of money allowed Obama to conduct mind-share branding on an enormous scale, even going so far as to buy a 30-minute infomercial on all of the major networks just weeks before the general election.

When you have the resources, you can advertise your brand over your competitors and they just can't keep up. This allows you to capture share of mind in your audience, *all other things being equal.* For example, as his campaign progressed Barack Obama was able to associate the word "change" with him and his candidacy through the constant reinforcement of this message. The notion here is that when the voting public thought of change in politics as usual, they would have thought Barack Obama. Most people would not want to spend too much mental energy questioning or looking for alternatives, and would therefore vote for him because of this association.

At this point in the election, most voters have already made up their minds about the polarizing issues that are important to them, so if you can associate your brand with the remaining key issues that resonate with your audience, then you will most likely get their votes. If both candidates (brands) offer essentially the same thing, then the one who has the most advertising (and therefore association) will likely win. When the general election came around, those people who had identified with a particular candidate's unique position (e.g., Pro-Life/Pro-Choice, taxes, etc.) were already in their candidate's camp and Obama and McCain were left fighting for the "uncommitted." Because these voters had not already settled on the issues that truly did distinguish between the two brands, they would likely fall in line with whatever candidate did a better job of convincing them on the remaining issues. Unfortunately for John McCain, both he and Barack Obama were saying basically the same thing on these remaining issues (e.g., presidential ability, judgment, and change in politics as usual), so any true differences were no longer readily apparent. Mind-share branding ruled the day and Obama sailed to an easy victory.

And if you don't have deep pockets?

So, if you have the resources, then you could be successful with mind-share branding. However, this is not true for most would-be marketers who want to rise to the top of their industries or professions. If you're like most people, you probably don't have the seemingly unlimited resources of entrenched competitors. You need another strategy.

When Obama first entered the Democratic primary, things were different for him. In fact, when Obama entered the Democratic Primary race, he was a comparative unknown. Yet Obama did take on, and ultimately prevail against, the established brand of Hillary Clinton by capturing the hearts of Democratic supporters ultimately propelling him to victory over John McCain in the general election. The question remains, how does an upstart brand capture this type of loyalty to move to market dominance? The market-leader brand typically has the advantage and the resources to bury you in a head-to-head match and this should have been no different. By most people's standards, Clinton should have buried Obama.

The Obama campaign realized that mind-share branding is not necessarily the best way to proceed initially, especially for an unknown brand taking on an entrenched brand.

The Obama campaign realized that mind-share branding is not necessarily the best way to proceed initially, especially for an unknown brand taking on an entrenched brand. Marketers will advise you that to be competitive, you need to establish a unique identity for your brand. Additionally, this unique identity must be something that people care about and emotionally invest in if you want to harness its true power. This notion, originally termed positioning, is the idea that your brand must offer some type of unique benefit to your audience in an overcrowded market.[11] In reality, this notion has been around for some time as the Unique Selling Proposition (USP) school of marketing (although many individuals and small business owners ignore even this; at their own peril). Positioning as a concept is actually quite straightforward. You and your brand need to be known for something unique and something that is valuable to your audience. If your competition can copy you, then it's not truly a unique advantage. It's not enough to say that your brand is "better" because nobody believes that anymore. Instead, you need to show tangible benefits that your audience will gain by purchasing your brand or doing business with you.

Positioning attempts to show the value of your brand to your target audience. Most brands mess this up though and don't put the value their brand delivers into something that resonates emotionally with their audience.

While the positioning aspect of branding is a good start for many organizations, it doesn't show the true power of how Barack Obama was as successful in his campaign as he was. Positioning attempts to show the value of your brand to your target audience. Most brands mess this up though, and don't put the value their brands deliver into something that resonates emotionally with their audience. Positioning has at its heart the idea of standing out in the mind of your audience, leading to consumers that are satisfied with your brand. However, satisfaction is not loyalty. To gain true loyalty your brand must appeal to somebody at a deeper, more emotional level than just their reasoning and logic as so often found in mind share branding. In order to have truly powerful branding, especially against an entrenched competitor, your brand must connect to your audience at this deeper level.[12] This is what the Obama campaign was able to do so successfully.

Building a strong and successful brand

There are many theories on what builds a truly strong and successful brand, but certain commonalities run throughout. Marketers have suggested for some time that powerful brands move your product from the rationally chosen commodity world to one of emotion and inspiration.[13] Rather than just abstract associations with attributes and benefits, a deeper, cultural connection is one that would be more beneficial to brands. Barack Obama took advantage of deeply imprinted cultural norms and psychology to gain his early market share.

Strong brands arise from strong identities. These identities can take different forms, with two of the forms being brand as person and brand as symbol (both of which Barack Obama successfully developed). Execution of the brand identity is created through symbols and metaphors, with a great deal of testing to determine those elements that have the most meaning to the consumer.[14] Barack Obama entered the race with a very strong personal story. Prior to his entry, he had already written two best-selling books and delivered the keynote speech at the 2004 Democratic Party Convention.[15] Obama was widely touted for his rhetorical ability and his use of story and metaphor to create mental images for his audience.[16] These abilities served him well because truly powerful brands have personality. If you want to attract passionate consumers, your brand must have a dynamic personality associated with it.[17]

This use of powerful story and symbolism helped him gain an audience but it wasn't the main reason he was as successful as he was. Barack Obama was able to take his brand from one that was emotionally appealing to one that achieved almost mythic, iconic proportions. Obama was often compared to a "rock star" due to the size and passion of the audiences he attracted. Even early in his campaign, Obama was often booked at venues over actual rock groups because of his ability to sell more tickets.[18] How does a brand create this level of passion among its audience? The reasons are as powerful as they are profound.

Barack Obama was often compared to a "rock star" due to the size and passion of the audiences he attracted. How does a brand create this level of passion within its audience?

Obama first started his campaign with the message of hope. While he did attack the status quo, he was careful to also phrase his speeches in terms of hopes and dreams. His appeal to common fears and attitudes of his audience, coupled with his tone of how things could be better helped set his campaign apart from many of his Democratic rivals. This is a rather common strategy among many politicians, so Obama took it a step further. Fear appeals by themselves, often are not enough to get people to take action or support your brand.[19] Instead of just making people fearful, you have to instead show them how the status quo is not fulfilling their dreams and destiny. In order to capture brand loyalty from competing brands, you need to identify a key, salient issue of discontent and talk about that instead. Barack Obama was able to do this with Hillary Clinton and later John McCain by painting both of them as Washington insiders and supporters of the Iraq war.[20]

Truly iconic brands lead culture rather than follow culture. By taking a provocative stand against the status quo, a marketer is able to show a contradiction of ideologies. Truly iconic brands don't become iconic unless and until they alienate people holding contradicting viewpoints.[21] This is imperative to understand especially in the realm of politics, where it is true that powerful enemies make for better fans. Obama was able to cast himself as the outsider taking on the powerful Washington elite (his own party included) thereby allowing his fans to join him on this almost mystical undertaking.[22]

> *Strong brands arise from strong identities. These identities can take different forms, with two of the forms being brand as person and brand as symbol (both of which Barack Obama successfully developed).*

Barack Obama took advantage of many classic marketing principles

While Obama would joke that his name was a disadvantage to his candidacy, in many ways it actually helped him for branding purposes. Many times being different is good for a brand. People are hardwired to detect irregular things, so something like a unique name can make you stand out from your competition and get you noticed.[23]

Other factors helped Barack Obama as well. For example, you can obtain a very successful emotional branding advantage if your audience sees you as the "new" entrant in a field. People are drawn to the word "new." By casting himself as a new form of politician, Barack Obama was able to take advantage of this simple principle. In this case, not being well-known on the national scene worked to his distinct advantage.[24] If your brand has no clear strengths, it is often better to cast off any negative connotations of what you are selling and recast yourself in a new light.[25]

Barack Obama also mastered the art of selling to and through people's beliefs. There is a cardinal rule in marketing we would all be well-advised to remember. Reality doesn't matter, only perception. Whatever your audience thinks and believes is true, is true to them. Marketing to and through people's beliefs is therefore another very powerful branding strategy. Beliefs are very rarely isolated but rather part of a system of beliefs. To change people's beliefs you must undermine their entire belief system, not just a single belief. Marketers need to remember that people will make decisions based on limited information and therefore will base their beliefs on the best information that is available. To be truly effective, remember that people often substitute fantasy for belief and wishes for wants and desires. Appealing to people's fantasies and wishes is a very effective branding strategy.[26]

> *There is a cardinal rule in marketing we would all be well-advised to remember. Reality doesn't matter, only perception. It's not what you think you are, it's what your audience thinks you are that actually matters!*

Throughout the campaign, the Obama team was able to understand and change his audiences' beliefs. His organization wisely chose to build his brand through the use of internet technology, thereby attracting distinct types of voters who had felt disenfranchised with the political process. The ingrained belief of many of these people was that they were tired of politics and politicians. Obama presented himself as not just another politician, but as a youthful alternative that could help affect the change these people sought.[27]

This allowed Obama to help his core audience fulfill the personal stories they found themselves living.[28] Being very popular among the youth vote, Obama was able to tap into a frustration and story that many of them felt about creating their own destiny and having an influence on how the government runs.[29] Indeed, early in his campaign some people criticized Obama for turning down an AARP sponsored candidate forum in favor of attending a hip-hop event.[30] The conventional wisdom had been that any candidate who actively courted and counted on the youth vote would lose the election. However, Obama successfully branded himself to the millennial generation and they in turn came out in droves to help him win key primary states as well as the general election.[31]

Truly successful brands don't just appeal to people's emotions, but gain absolute loyalty of the audience by appealing to the stories that we all tell ourselves. When a brand allows your audience to interpret the meaning in their lives, you will get their loyal support where your competitors will not.[32]

Barack Obama and his campaign successfully managed to come from a relative unknown position and take on the predominant brands in politics. Through the application of classic marketing principles, he rose to the top of his field. Through the application of classic marketing principles, you can as well.

Marketing implications of this chapter:

- First and foremost, you must establish an identity for your brand that differentiates you from your competition. While seemingly obvious, many individuals and small businesses are not able to adequately describe who they are and what they do that is different from anybody else. If your market cannot distinguish you from your competition, they have no reason to seek you out or support your brand. They probably don't even know who you are!

- The steps to branding are actually quite simple to understand, but not so simple to implement effectively. Briefly, you need to:

  - Determine if your target audience is already aware of you.

  - If your target audience doesn't know who you are: begin branding! If your target audience knows who you are, find out what they think of you.

  - Decide on the type of brand you would like to be. What is your identity?

- Implement your branding campaign while following the 5 C's of branding

  - Are all of your brand elements Clear?

  - Are all of your brand elements Connected?

  - Are all of your brand elements Complementary (e.g., internet, radio, storefront, etc.)?

  - Are all of your brand elements presenting a Comprehensive view of your brand?

  - Are all of your brand elements Consistently delivered and reinforced (and no, we're not just talking about advertising here)?

- Merely running ads or other promotions that tell your name may build some brand awareness, but it won't sell anything for you. Many individuals and small business owners make the mistake of believing that merely putting their name in front of their audience is enough to drive business. It's not! Unless you have the resources to repeat your message so often that people think of you when they think of your product category, advertising your name with no value statement is most likely a waste of resources.

- Many people feel that they do not have enough control in their lives. Because of this frustration people have a desire to control their lives, with resulting discrepancies of what they want versus what they don't have. Understanding and appealing to this innate desire for control can make your brand very successful.

- The excitement and discovery of the new motivates many people. Those who thought they were discovering Barack Obama became very excited about him and were more than willing to share their thoughts and discoveries with their friends. If you can think of ways to position your brand as something new and exciting, you can set up opportunities for your audience to "discover" and share your brand.[33]

- Many people have the innate need for belonging to something, especially among the millennial generation. If your brand can successfully make people feel that they are part of your community, and/or a community of like-minded individuals, then you have a very powerful brand on your hands.

- Self actualization is also an important emotional appeal for a brand. People have a natural desire to aspire towards self-fulfillment after their more basic needs have been met. Therefore, if you're able to appeal to the better notions within people, then you can have a great deal of emotional impact on your customers.

- A chance to start over with a clean slate is emotionally satisfying to many people by sweeping out the old and bringing in the new. This was especially prevalent with Obama, when he made the case that it should be no more politics as usual, but time for a fresh beginning where everybody could play together in the realm of politics. If you can think of ways to peg your entrenched competition as part of an old system, you can have a chance of sweeping them away with your new approach.

- Everything else being equal, it is often much more appealing to build your brand on positive conditions and to not directly attack or hurt your competition.[34] Stress the unique value that your brand offers along with the emotional benefits people get from doing business with you.

- Successful brands should be clear and concise in their messages and think of branding in terms of public relations, not advertising. This allows your brand to come across as human which will be more appealing to your audience.

- Most important of all: It's not what you think you are, it's what the audience thinks you are that actually matters. Always poll your audience to see if the message they are receiving about your brand is the one you think you are (and want to be) giving.

CHAPTER 3

An Introduction to the BARACK
Marketing System

Barack Obama was elected President of the United States because he and his campaign followed classic principles of marketing and branding. While many of Obama's competitors were left wondering how he overpowered them, the reality is that he followed a system that, when successfully deployed, will almost always ensure victory for the marketer.

The good news is that anybody can follow this same system, if only you know and use these classic techniques. The remainder of this book will show you how Obama succeeded by following six marketing principles and how you can do the same in your business or personal life. Each step will be discussed with examples from Barack Obama and his campaign. The marketing principles that were successfully used will be identified and you will learn how to use these same principles in your own marketing efforts.

Barack Obama was elected President of the United States because he and his campaign followed classic principles of marketing and branding.

Once he decided to enter the presidential race, Barack Obama never doubted that he could win. As you will see this belief in yourself is of fundamental importance whenever you wish to dominate your market. However, belief is not enough. You also need to conduct thorough market research and fully understand your customers. Obama's early days as community organizer provided him with the tools he needed to understand the motivations of his audience. If you wish to succeed in business today, you will need an understanding of basic consumer behavior and what makes people tick, as well as what they strongly desire.

In addition, you need to hold a clearly defined role in the mind of your customer. Your customers need to believe your story and see how your story intersects with their own personal stories. Your audience needs to see you as their spokesperson; their champion. You must learn to position yourself in the minds of your customers as the ONLY possible solution to the problems they are facing. This is actually a relatively simple technique that is mastered by few. Obama mastered this technique and you can as well.

However, it's not enough to merely have a defined role for your audience; you need for your role to be one that is highly desired by your audience as well. You, the marketer, need to understand and tap into the cultural angst that your audience is feeling. You must understand the conflicts your audience feel and learn how to tap into their deepest psychological yearnings. Barack Obama successfully understood and gave voice to the aspirations of his audience, propelling him to victory. You can use these same techniques to help propel you to the top of your field.

Once you've successfully identified your strategy for each of these steps, you need to be sure that all of your marketing messages communicate the same strategy. Obama and his campaign learned how to create this congruence and you can as well.

Lastly, Barack Obama was one of the first politicians to take full advantage of internet marketing and all of the power that provides. He successfully identified his community and was able to ignite them to act with unprecedented speed and passion. You will see how to identify your community and how you can position yourself to take advantage of internet speed in your marketing efforts.

These six classic principles that Obama used in his presidential campaign can be summarized and remembered by the following acronym:

Belief in yourself

Audience understanding

Role identification

Aspiration delivery

Congruence of tactics

Kindle your community

With these six principles in mind, you will be able to employ the strategy and tactics that will propel you to the top of your field. So, turn the page and learn how to BARACK your competition!

CHAPTER 4

Step 1: Belief in Yourself

There is an unspoken rule among successful marketers; if you don't truly believe that what you are selling is of the utmost importance to your customers, then don't sell it. Successful marketers believe deep in their bones that the world (or at least their target audience) truly benefits from what we offer. Successful marketers love their customers and want to provide as much value to them as possible.

The logic follows, if you truly love your customers and want what is best for them, then you must also truly believe that you are the only viable source to deliver it to them. In essence, by not selling your goods and services to the customers you profess to love you are actually doing them a disservice. Successful business people must believe in themselves every bit as much as Barack Obama did throughout his election.

The marketing process can be summarized by the simple statement of "value exchange." What this tells us is that if you want people to give you something of value, then you must give them something of value first. If you want people to give you more value (e.g., money or votes) then you must promise your audience even greater value than your competition does. And if you don't believe that what you are offering your audience is more valuable then what your competition is offering, then really, why should someone buy what you're selling?

At the end of the day, all wildly successful business people (as well as politicians, actors and others) have a certain amount of arrogance about them. It takes a great deal of confidence and belief in self to launch a successful campaign whether it is political or business. Most importantly though, your audience must see the value behind what you're offering.

If and when they do, then they will support you in your efforts. Barack Obama mastered the art of self-confidence in his political career. He exuded this confidence to his audience and they began to believe in him also. This first step is a necessary condition for you to succeed as well. Continue reading to learn how Obama did this and what you need to do if you desire massive success.

> *At the end of the day, all wildly successful business people (as well as politicians, actors, and others) have a certain amount of arrogance about them. It takes a great deal of confidence and belief in self to launch a successful campaign whether it is political or business. Do you have what it takes?*

CHAPTER 5

Marketer's Psychology

"In a country of 300 million people, there is a certain degree of audacity required for anybody to say, "I'm the best person to lead this country."

Barack Obama, *Washington Post*, Nov. 18, 2006

Marketing lives in the mind. The simple economics of supply and demand we all learned are true as long as we have competition. Successful marketers understand this and therefore we do everything in our power to eliminate competition. When your public sees you as being interchangeable, there is no inherent reason to select you over your competition other than price and availability. The interesting thing is that it doesn't matter whether or not you actually are better than your competition; if your market doesn't see the difference then there is none!

Politicians and business people will always fight for competitive advantage. This is that unique "something" you have to provide your audience that no other competitor has. We have discussed how this could be more and better resources that allow you to outspend on advertising or price consistently lower than your competition or some type of unique technology that you have and your competition doesn't (e.g., a patent for something that is desired by the market).

The reality though is that you probably don't have more resources or truly unique technologies than your competition does. You are left with the option of out-marketing your competition if you want to thrive. And the only way to truly out-market your competition is to convince your audience that your competition is not actually your competition! Namely, you have to convince your audience that you are a product of one; if they want what you have to offer then they have no choice but to do business with you. Nobody can do what you do as well as you do it. Your audience has to believe this and **you** have to believe it as well!

You need a strong ego

A strong ego is crucial for success in politics and the marketplace. As Barack Obama wrote in <u>The Audacity of Hope</u>: *"Few people end up being United States senators by accident; at a minimum, it requires a certain megalomania, a belief that of all the gifted people in your state, you are somehow uniquely qualified to speak on their behalf; a belief sufficiently strong that you are willing to endure the sometimes uplifting, occasionally harrowing, but always slightly ridiculous process we call campaigns."*[35]

Whether you agree with Barack Obama's viewpoints or not, few would argue that he has a great deal of belief in them. It was often said throughout the campaign that Obama was almost too confident to the point of being cocky. While this may not be an effective strategy for many people, the underlying principle is sound; you must convince your audience that you believe in yourself before they will believe in you.

The "presence" of Barack Obama was often cited as a reason for support throughout the campaign. Some would call him arrogant; others would call him confident. His self-assuredness could be seen as cocky to his detractors and calming to his supporters. Yet regardless of which side voters fell out on, most would agree that Obama surely believed he was the best and most qualified candidate to be President and exuded this (choose one) brash/calming, confident/arrogant demeanor throughout his campaign.

> *It was often said throughout the campaign that Obama was almost too confident to the point of being cocky. While this may not be an effective strategy for many people, the underlying principle is sound; you must convince your audience that you believe in yourself before they will believe in you.*

Barack Obama always exhibited extreme self-confidence

Pundits who studied the Obama campaign point out three specific examples of Obama's extreme self-confidence: 1) He announced his Presidential bid with only two years of national service; 2) He didn't "wait his turn" when he challenged Hillary Clinton in the Democratic primaries; 3) During the general election he modeled ex-presidents by hosting a rally in Berlin and created a campaign seal that looked almost exactly like the presidential seal.[36] These last actions led to him being labeled as "the anointed one" by his detractors and "presidential" by his supporters[37], but nonetheless show that the man possesses a very strong ego.

Even one of Barack Obama's closest advisors, David Plouffe, reported of Obama's extreme self-confidence at one of their very early presidential exploration meetings. Plouffe describes Obama's reaction, typical of many entrepreneurs, to letting go of some of the day-to-day management of his campaign when Obama tells him, "*...this is my life and my career. And I think I could probably do every job on the campaign better than the people I'll hire to do it....*"[38] This attitude is very typical of successful business owners. Not to say that you won't have to let go of some control at some point in your business, but a successful marketer truly believes that what he or she does is important and that he/she is the absolute best person in the world to deliver on the promise.

In management and marketing you will often hear of the term "expectancy." Basically, this suggests that people will tend to attract what they expect. While there are several different theories about how this exactly works,[39] the basic notion of self-fulfilling prophecies can hold in business. The laws of attraction suggest that you draw those things to you that you think about the most.[40] If you are constantly thinking of ways to benefit your audience and why you OWE it to your constituents or clients to sell them what you have to offer, then you are well on your way to developing the supreme self-confidence that truly successful marketers have.

The psychology of the customer

Successful marketers are aware that there is only one radio station that all people consistently listen to: WIIFM. This is the station "What's In It For Me?" Although politicians and business owners may not like to hear or believe it, your customers don't care about you and why you are in business. They only care about themselves and how you can benefit them. Later, they may come to care about you but only in the context of how whatever you do can benefit their lives. So, the first step to successful marketing is that you must convince your audience that whatever you offer is of such unique value to them that they can't live without it. And, in order to accomplish this you must act from a position of love for what you do and the benefits that your audience will obtain from doing business with you.

Successful marketers believe in the very fiber of their beings that what they offer is so unique and worthwhile that their audience would be crazy to not take advantage of it. With this mindset you have an obligation to sell whatever you sell to your customers because you know, deep in your heart, that they will be worse off without what you are offering.[41] Essentially you are saying, "you must have this and I won't take no for an answer!" When you believe this you will always and consistently put your customer's needs ahead of your own. You don't want to just sell somebody a product or service to benefit yourself; you have to believe in your heart that what you offer is so unique and worthwhile to your audience that you are the only logical choice for them to do business with.

Although politicians and business owners may not like to hear or believe it, your customers don't care about you and why you are in business. People are only interested in the station WIIFM, "What's In It For Me?" If you don't see the value in what you're offering, then your audience most certainly won't!

When you are seeking something for yourself, wouldn't you like a trusted friend to help you in the search? Somebody who you believe has YOUR best interests at heart and not their own? Well, your audience wants the exact same thing from the people they do business with, whether it be a politician or a florist.[42]

If you are looking to take advantage of your audience, they will eventually figure it out. If you are saying to yourself, "I'm going to sell them a bill of goods" and you don't actively believe what you are offering is of true value, your audience will suspect it and drop you like a 10-pound weight. But, if you really do believe in what you're offering to your audience, then they will sense this as well and listen to you.

People have an uncanny ability to detect confidence in others. Your first step to branding success is to have confidence in yourself.

Marketing implications of this chapter:

- To be ultimately successful in building your brand, it is crucial to think of the ways your audience could benefit from choosing you.

- Remember, at the end of the day your audience doesn't really care about why you are in business but rather what's in it for them. Don't tell your audience how wonderful you are, but show them how wonderful you are by appealing to their own self-interest.

- In order to get your audience to believe in you, you must truly believe that you are unique in what you offer and that no one else can match you in terms of what you deliver.

- Realize that not everybody will agree with you in your belief of being the best at what you do. That's alright. Expect your competition to not agree with you. The key is to get your target audience to agree with you.

CHAPTER 6

Step 2: Audience Understanding

While belief in yourself is an essential first step to successful marketing and branding efforts, it is by no means sufficient. As we discussed, to be truly successful your target audience has to believe in you as well. If they don't, then you will merely be seen as arrogant and cocky and will most likely be derided rather than applauded. The second step in the **BARACK *Marketing System*** is **Audience Understanding.**

In today's fragmented market, no one person, organization, or brand will be loved by all people. There are far too many differences in the population to believe that one answer will fit all. This is not a bad thing though. The trick is to correctly identify your target market and to make whatever you are offering appear invaluable to them. Understanding consumer behavior and market segmentation is a crucial first step to effectively develop your brand's position in the mind of your audience.

People are needs and wants driven by nature. Successful marketers do not attempt to force themselves and their products on their audience, but rather find out what their potential audience wants first. Market research at this step is essential. If you don't know what is motivating your target audience and what value they seek from a relationship with you, then you most likely won't last long in your interactions with them.

Unfortunately, many individuals and business people think in terms of their own interests rather than their audience's. As discussed, this might result in short-term profits, but most likely will not be a successful long term strategy. We are all motivated by our self-interests, whether they are tangible or intangible. Successful marketers will always take the pulse of their audience to see what, exactly, is motivating them to action and what they desire.

The days of mass marketing are long gone and out of

reach for most individuals and small business owners. **While some would argue that Barack Obama attempted to appeal to all (a mass marketing approach) in reality he did quite the opposite. Obama correctly understood that in order to come from nowhere he had to completely understand what motivated his core audience and determine a way to promise it to them.** To be successful, you need to do this as well.

CHAPTER 7

Uncovering Your Audience's Deepest Desires

"Find out their self-interest, he said. That's why people become involved in organizing - because they think they'll get something out of it. Once I found an issue enough people cared about, I could take them into action. With enough actions, I could start to build power."

Barack Obama from
Dreams From My Father: A Story of Race and Inheritance [43]

Consumers are overwhelmed. Every day thousands of advertising messages bombard us, threatening to bury us with their persistent hype and (mis)information. Which brand of cola should I buy? What type of car should I drive? Who should I vote for? Our modern lives are hectic and most people do not have a great deal of time to research, let alone understand all of our options. We need shortcuts. Usually the shortcut involves selecting the familiar, something we've heard of. Unknown brands have an uphill battle when challenging an incumbent brand merely because most people have never heard of, and therefore will never consider, you. To succeed, you must break through the clutter and quickly capture the attention and loyalty of your audience.

Uncovering your audience's desires

Principles that were true 3000 years ago are essentially true today. People don't do things without motivation. Motivation might be as simple as feeling the need to eat because you are hungry to something as complex as running for elected office because you want to make a difference in the world. Marketers will talk about consumers as being bundles of needs and wants. Find a need and fill it. That's the key to success. Consumers are motivated to fulfill their needs and wants. Successful marketing shows solutions to the problems that your audience is facing. When you as the marketer show your audience that they are having a problem and you are the solution to their problem, they will buy whatever you are offering and both sides win. Everybody's happy.

While there is a great deal of truth to these ideas, they do not tell the entire story. Today's consumers are much more skeptical than consumers of 50 years ago. The internet generation expects immediate answers and satisfaction. Forget snail mail, you had better answer me within the hour! Yes, consumers will still look for people and products that solve their problems, but today's marketer, more than ever, must understand what is really motivating his audience and gain their trust in order to gain their loyalty. If you wish to be a successful marketer, you first and foremost must understand what motivates your audience and what their true needs and wants are. From there, you can build an effective marketing campaign that will propel you to victory.

Steps to a successful marketing campaign

The Obama campaign intuitively understood the steps to a successful marketing campaign. These steps are:

1. Identify the true needs and wants of your audience.
2. Identify the environment you are selling in.
3. Survey your competition to see what they are offering.
4. Find a hole in the competition; an audience need that is not being met.
5. Identify what you have to offer. What strengths and advantages do you bring to the table?
6. Match your strengths to the audiences' unmet and most desired needs.
7. Get the word out and watch your sales grow.

While these steps obviously simplify a much longer and involved process, the fundamentals remain the same. Barack Obama successfully navigated the political waters by adroitly using these marketing principles. Understanding what motivates his core constituents was the first step on his road to victory.

Everyone likes to think that they make rational decisions when purchasing, yet nothing could be further from the truth. Consumers like to believe that they think about the purchases they make in a logical and thoughtful manner, but this is seldom the case. Ask anyone in sales and they will tell you that people buy on emotion and justify with reason.[44] Even if a consumer does "think" about her purchase, chances are good that she has used mental shortcuts to help make her job easier. The bottom line is that thinking is hard work for most people, so most people don't actually really do it! While you might make a sale or two appealing to people's logic, the way to garner their loyalty is to sell to their emotion.[45]

If you wish to be a successful marketer, you first and foremost must understand what motivates your audience and what their true needs and wants are. From there you can build an effective marketing campaign that will propel you to victory.

Marketers need to get at the heart of what motivates their audience in order to gain their support. Effective marketing and sales programs always begin with consumer wants first and foremost. Delivering the best solution to your audience, in a subconscious and shorthand manner, is usually the best route to gain attention and ultimately the purchases and loyalty of your audience.

Early in his political career, Barack Obama learned how to understand his audience and probe for what mattered the most to them. As a community organizer, Obama quickly learned what did and did not matter to the people he was working with. The streets of Chicago provided ample opportunity for Obama to talk with would-be voters about problems they faced and solutions they wanted. As he quickly learned, it wasn't enough to stop at the surface level of probing, as so many marketers do, but to push people to the deeper problems that they faced and how these impacted their lives. Obama expressed this best in his own words when describing his days as a community organizer: *"If you want to organize people, you need to steer away from the peripheral stuff and go towards people's centers. The stuff that makes them tick. Otherwise, you'll never form the relationships you need to get them involved."* [46]

What Obama discovered was that people seldom tell you what is really motivating them when you first ask them about it. Your audience isn't necessarily lying to you, they may simply not know. Motives tend to be hidden from view and most people cannot accurately put into words what they really think or feel.[47] People tend to think in images and metaphors, not words. Successful marketers learn to get past the initial responses of their audience to discover what is truly motivating the consumer.[48]

Understanding your audience's environment

Learning what people really think, feel and desire is the first step to successful branding. Business doesn't take place in a vacuum though. A major impact on you and your audience is the environment that surrounds us. Environmental factors in marketing can take on many forms, from technology and economic impacts to socio-cultural and political. A successful politician, like any successful marketer, will constantly be scanning the environment for how it's impacting people. What makes a truly successful politician or marketer though is to once more go past the surface impact of the environment and look at what is truly happening in our culture and society. Deep impact issues are ones that hit people at their core. These issues and concerns are the ones that cause people to question their hopes and beliefs at a very profound level.[49] Through his interviews with constituents, combined with his own beliefs, Obama was able to identify several deep impact issues that made him popular amongst his target audience. The ability to show the impact of these issues on his audience, while suggesting that he was the only one who understood the issues, put him in a very powerful position. As an example, Obama was one of the first politicians to speak out against the war in Iraq and the response to Hurricane Katrina.[50] Both the war and Katrina were external events that affected the lives of Americans. Obama recognized that many of his constituents felt disenfranchised due to the actions of the government and it was this sense of disconnection he spoke of in his speeches.

What is your competitive advantage?

Once you understand your audience's needs both at a personal and environmental level, it is time to survey the competitive landscape and see what others are selling. Given the slate of offerings that are available to your audience, you must determine where you fit in the landscape. The easiest way to do this is to first understand the three ways that marketers can create an advantage and decide how you can and should compete.

Successful marketers identify advantages they have over their competition that make their audience want to do business with them. Ideally, these advantages are unique to you and not easily copied by others. Uniqueness is important. While there are countless variations of competitive advantage, in reality there are only three sources for all of them.

First is a resource advantage. When you have a resource advantage you basically have more resources (e.g., money or distribution channels) than does your competition. If you are so lucky as to be the top dog in the market, it will be very hard for any of your competition to come close to touching you because ultimately you can just outspend them.

When Obama first entered the Democratic Primary race, he had to take on several seasoned and well-funded competitors. At that time, Hillary Clinton was the presumptive nominee and had the financial backing and name recognition that Obama did not.[51] Her war chest and 20 years of experience made her the market leader of the time. Through the strategic use of powerful social marketing and fundraising efforts Obama was able to raise a war chest very rapidly allowing him to quickly overwhelm his opponents with advertising and other promotions. Once Obama became the Democratic nominee, his name recognition and fundraising prowess allowed him an enormous resource advantage over John McCain, his opponent in the general election, allowing him to buy commercial airtime and other promotions that McCain could not even come close to matching.[52]

> *Successful marketers understand that there are only three sources of competitive advantage you can have: 1) You have more money or other resources than your competition; 2) You have some type of desired knowledge or technology that your competition doesn't have; 3) You are a better marketer.*

> *While Barack Obama acquired money (and plenty of it) throughout his campaign, the true key to his success was that he was a better marketer than his competition.*

Entering the race, Obama faced the problem that many Democrats had not heard of him and would likely vote for Clinton out of habit and familiarity, if nothing else.[53] Obama needed to get Democrats, and later Republicans and Independents, to consider voting for him rather than their own front-runner candidates. This he accomplished by suggesting that "insider" politicians in general had violated the trust of the American public, and that it was time for a change.[54] Being a master at understanding context and the psychology of the market, the Obama campaign was able to take many opportunities that might have spelled disaster for other candidates and turn them into political hay, i.e., political contributions.[55] While not starting with a resource advantage, soundly applied marketing led to Obama quickly gaining one.

The second advantage an organization or person can have is technology. Simply put, a technology advantage would mean that you own some form of knowledge or technology that your competition doesn't, such as a patented system or great expertise. Clinton's campaign and later McCain's attempted to brand Obama as not having enough experience to win the election or be president.[56] These campaigns were positioning their candidates as having more experience and expertise than Obama, or essentially, as possessing a technology that Obama did not have. While this may indeed have been true, these charges did not work against Obama. Why? Because Barack Obama had mastered the third competitive advantage from the inception of his campaign; a marketing advantage.

Power comes from a marketing advantage. People and organizations that truly understand the power of marketing can, and usually do, beat the competition holding either a resource or technology advantage. The ultimate truth of branding and marketing is that, at the end of the day, reality doesn't matter. Whatever your audience perceives to be true is true to them. If company X does indeed have a technology advantage over you, but your customers don't see the need for that technology or believe that you can deliver on that technology just as well (whether true or not), you will win. Obama's supporters obviously did believe that their candidate was presidential material, so this technology advantage of Clinton and McCain became a moot point. Lesson learned; marketing prevails. If you can capture the hearts, minds, and loyalty of your audience then it doesn't matter if your competition has a resource or technology advantage. Your audience will stay loyal to you.

On the other hand, if your audience is not committed to you, there is a great deal of risk you will lose them to your competition with a resource or technology advantage. Once again, the importance of Obama being able to quickly capture the loyalty of his audience and rapidly grow his customer base contributed to his success. When first starting out, Barack

Obama had to convince members of the Democratic Party why they should select him over the other, better-known, Democratic candidates.

> **Obama's supporters obviously did believe that their candidate was presidential material, so the technology advantage of Clinton and McCain (i.e., experience) became a moot point. Lesson learned; marketing prevails.**

Identifying your competitive advantage

Fortunately for Barack Obama, he understood that most people define their competitive advantage incorrectly. It is all too common for many brands to position themselves as either the "me-too" or "alternative" candidate. Neither of these is necessarily a very effective strategy. By being a me-too candidate in the sense of yes "I believe what my opponent believes" the candidate that is better-known or first to market will typically win. While this might be advantageous if you are first or better-known, it is disastrous if you are not. Another common mistake is for people to position themselves as the alternative candidate. This position oftentimes is not much better than the "me-too" position. Essentially this position says; whatever candidate X is, I am not. The problem with the alternative position is that you are asking people to vote for you merely because you are not your opponent. While this strategy may sometimes prove effective in politics, it surely is not the most effective strategy to gain loyal ardent supporters. Barack Obama inherently realized this by not appealing to the antithesis positions but rather to new goals and dreams to which his supporters subscribed.[57] Successful marketers will study their competition to discover their strengths, as well as the inherent weakness in their strengths. From this, the successful marketer will identify one or two relevant points that are not being addressed by their entrenched competition and make these the focal point of marketing efforts. In order to capture brand loyalty from competing brands, you need to identify a key, salient issue and talk about that instead. Barack Obama was able to do this with Hillary Clinton and later John McCain by painting both of them as Washington insiders and supporters of the Iraq war.[58] Through this process, Obama was able to successfully create a value proposition for his audience that took advantage of people's natural tendency to want to support an ideal state.[59]

Looking at your strengths and your opponents weaknesses

Having identified the other Democratic contenders weaknesses (as well as the weaknesses with the Republicans and the election process in general) Obama pounced. A key hole that Obama discovered and used was the use of internet technology to spread his message and gain financial support. His use of new technology, considered to be the most adept of any candidate, allowed him to build organized volunteer armies across the states.[60] In addition, Obama targeted a voting bloc that was essentially ignored by most politicians – the youth vote. Obama played to the ideals of Millennials, a key group of voters in his eventual victories. The younger voter believed that everybody had a role to play and these voters were naturally inclined to be unified. This mindset made them very receptive to Obama's messages of inclusion, unity, and change.[61] In fact, the youth vote identified by the Obama campaign was instrumental to his early victories in the Democratic primaries. Under 25-year olds voted for Obama at a rate of 4-1 over his nearest competitors in the Iowa caucuses. It was this vote that was credited for propelling him to victory over Hillary Clinton and giving him the credibility and momentum he needed for the rest of the primary.[62]

Obama also recognized the powerful use of story and metaphor in his rhetoric and was able to connect with his audiences in a manner that his opponents could not.[63] Last, his identification of change and turmoil in our culture, as well as his exploitation of the same, propelled him and his message to the top of the field.[64]

Obama had spent much time in introspection of who he

was, and had even written a best-selling memoir detailing his thoughts.[65] This assessment of his strengths and weaknesses allowed him to develop his own distinctive voice. He used this voice to position him in the political opening he saw. Billing himself as *"...a tall, skinny guy with big ears and a funny name"*[66] Obama was able to tell stories about himself and his vision to an ever-growing and adoring audience.

Truly dominating your market requires upstarts and unknowns to start small and grow big – fast! Of course, this is all relative to the size of your market, but the goal of being the big player in your market remains. Obama started by first courting those constituents who were most likely to believe in and receive his message. His strong personality allowed his supporters to connect with him on an almost visceral level.[67] While he did appeal to a certain amount of fear[68], Obama mostly kept his campaign focused on "hope" and "change" thereby appealing to people's better nature and optimism.[69] This in turn helped create more loyal fans that would go out of their way to spread his message and work to advance his candidacy.[70] Once he was able to achieve critical mass, his message spread like wildfire, propelling him to victory.

Marketing implications of this chapter:

- If you want to dominate your market, you must first determine exactly what that market is. The days of mass marketing for the small business or individual are over. Barack Obama started on the streets of Chicago to learn what motivated his audience. You need to start with a small, defined market and learn everything you can about them first, before expanding your operation, if you'd like to increase your chances of success.

- It is not enough to ask only surface questions of your prospective customers. Most people cannot readily identify what it is that motivates them, even if they were inclined to tell you in the first place! You must be sure to ask follow-up questions and probe your market to identify deeper meanings.

- Remember that most people have a great deal of difficulty expressing themselves in words. Techniques such as laddering and metaphor elicitation can be of great benefit to you when uncovering hidden meaning.

- Environmental scanning is the process of looking at what is going on in your audience's environment. It is comprised of understanding economic, socio-cultural, technological, political, and competitive factors. A very effective way of looking at your environment is to list what is happening and what is likely/possible to happen to your market. Then, plan a response for each of these scenarios so that you are ready when the time is right.

- Barack Obama was a master at identifying not only environmental factors, but looking at the psychological implications of these factors on his audience. Successful marketers don't just look at the situation affecting their audience, but put the ramifications of the situation into concrete terms and problems their audience face. This is exactly what Barack Obama did when he first began organizing in Chicago discussing gang violence.[71] To be truly effective, it's best to be specific with your audience.

- Take a close look at your competition. Identify what they are strongest at. Then, find the inherent weakness in their strength and see how you can use that to your advantage. Obama had to overcome the Clinton machine when he first entered the race. The strength of the Clinton machine was that it had a great deal of brand awareness with the public and was very large and well-known. The weakness in this was that Hillary Clinton by necessity had a long history with the American Public and could be seen as part of the "old" regime. Obama was able to position himself as the new and fresh alternative, rather than politics as usual, for an audience that had grown tired of ALL politicians.

- What do your more entrenched competitors do well?

- What is the weakness in that?

- How can you define your brand as addressing this inherent weakness?

- Decide what type of competitive advantage you want to use. For most individuals and small businesses, you won't have a resource advantage; at least not initially. If you are taking on a larger, better-funded competitor it becomes even more important for you to identify yourself with a story that resonates with your audience.

- Create a value proposition for your audience. Value propositions are a marketer's best friend. Ultimately all customers think in terms of the value that you can provide them with your product or service. Essentially value considers two aspects; the benefits received from purchasing and using a service or product, and the cost incurred when a service or product is purchased and used. Whenever people evaluate alternatives, they are always looking at the value that the various alternatives can provide them. Everything else being equal, the alternative that provides the most value will prevail at the end of the day. Assuming that people have more than one alternative to consider, they will choose the one that provides the best return on their investment. The costs involved and the value equation are more than just a physical product cost or price of something. The cost involved is a number of psychological social and economic factors that influence how much pain a person will suffer through acquisition and ownership or use of a product. Your benefit has to outweigh this pain, or you will not be successful.

- People no longer believe what can be called the '-er' promises. These are the promises of my product is better, my prices are cheaper, my product is faster, etc. Many organizations position themselves as better, faster, cheaper, which only serves to show your audience that you don't really stand for anything. Bottom line: people don't believe you.

- It is important to thoroughly understand your customer before you begin selling to them. Ask your audience the following types of questions:

  - What keeps them up at night?

  - What do they desire above all else?

  - What are they afraid of or angry about?

  - What trends are occurring that will affect your audience?

  - What are their top frustrations?

CHAPTER 8

Step 3: Role Identification

The greatest brands in the world have something in common. They all have a story to tell. People are story-driven. Whenever we hear a good story, we are willing to suspend disbelief while listening to and remembering what it is we're being told by the storyteller. Successful marketers recognize this, and so the most successful brands tell a story. While the other steps of the **BARACK Marketing System** are important, the most crucial one to creating a valuable and enduring brand is the correct identification and use of your role. Correct **Role Identification** will enable you to relate to your audience on a deep and profound level.

> **The greatest brands in the world have something in common. They all have a story to tell.**

Central to telling a story is for you (or your brand) to have a clearly defined role in the mind of your audience in the story. When your audience believes your character and cannot separate you from your character in their mind, then you own them. It's like the television star who becomes so closely identified with the role they play on TV that when people see them on the street they talk to them as if the actor is the character she plays rather than the person playing the character. This role identification makes your carefully crafted character indistinguishable from your brand. When done properly, this association of you with your character will lead your audience to attribute your character's authority to their own personal stories.

Barack Obama successfully identified himself as a character playing a role. He carefully crafted and portrayed his story throughout years of writing and speaking. By taking simple steps, Obama was able to own this role in the mind of the market making his competition appear to be copycats. The wonderful thing about role identification is that once done (and done properly) you will own this role in the mind of your market.

This section will explore how storytelling principles work in the mind of your audience and how Obama used them. You will also learn how Barack Obama portrayed a character based on universal and timeless appeals; appeals that people are hardwired to listen to. You will see how Obama cast himself as central to the stories that his audience tells themselves daily, becoming part of their personal narrative. This step alone made him seem indispensible to his core audience. This section will show you how he used these ideas to position himself to his core audience on a subconscious level; appearing to them as the classic hero, the only one in the world qualified to lead them. You will learn how Barack Obama positioned his product (i.e., himself) as a prop to the personal story that his audience was living, entwining his success with theirs.

Although it might appear so, there really is nothing magical about these steps. The key is to understand and apply them. So let's begin!

CHAPTER 9

The Art of the Story

"I stand here knowing that my story is part of the larger American story, that I owe a debt to all of those who came before me, and that, in no other country on earth, is my story even possible."

Barack Obama delivering the keynote address at
2004 democratic convention

Humans have always been fascinated by story. All cultures have at their root, a storytelling tradition. It is literally in our DNA, this fascination with a good story.[72]   When humans began communicating with each other, they did so with stories. For most people some of our earliest memories involve listening to stories told at bedtime or around the campfire. Stories helped us learn right from wrong and what our place in the world is.

Stories have been told for over 100,000 years whereas written communication began only six or seven thousand years ago. Considering that the populations of most Western cultures only began to read en masse a few hundred years ago it can be seen that the oral story tradition has been used throughout human history to convey ideas and cultural norms. In fact, every culture on the planet has a history of having created stories, fables, legend, and folk tales to convey their traditions and values. While not all cultures have developed logic, story is a common thread across humanity. Information presented in stories, and the stories themselves, are remembered longer than the same information presented in any other narrative form.[73]

Story and story structure

The stories that we know and love can find their roots in Greek myth. This is no accident as these myths came about through a process of trial and error when storytellers of old would tell their stories to the citizens. If you were a good storyteller and the people liked you, you would be rewarded with food and shelter. If the audience did not like your stories, then you would receive no such reward. Obviously, it was in the storyteller's better interest to tell stories that appealed to the population. Therefore, stories and story structure were essentially voted on by the marketplace of the day. This led to common story structure that we still see today. In truth, there are not really any original stories (at least ones that have mass appeal). Most stories that we know and respond to can trace their roots to the structures developed thousands of years ago. Given this, it is no surprise that story and story structure have been analyzed and used for generations. Philosophers since the days of Pythagoras and Socrates have looked at common themes that appealing stories possess, for it is in our stories that we show our culture.[74] The stories that we know today all consist of a few common structural elements found universally in myths, fairy tales, dreams and movies.[75] It is this universal and timeless nature of story which makes it so compelling and powerful for your audience.

> **Stories and storytelling structure have been around for thousands of years. We are essentially 'hardwired' to listen to and understand good stories. It should be no surprise then that the best storytellers (and marketers) are aware of and use proven techniques in their stories.**

While professional storytellers might disagree on the actual number, nearly all will agree that there are only a finite set of plots and structures that make for successful storytelling. A quick trip to the local cineplex will prove this point. How many times have we seen a variation on 'boy meets girl' or 'buddy adventure' films to realize that there really is nothing new under the sun? In fact, perhaps the most classic type of story structure that we all know is the hero's journey. Popularized by Joseph Campbell[76], the hero's journey discusses a story structure that is common across all cultures and their myths. The 'hero' starts his/her life in the ordinary world where he/she is just a regular person. Something happens (a 'call to action') that propels our heroes out of their comfort zones and forces them into a high-stakes adventure. While this call may be initially refused, the hero soon discovers that he or she cannot ignore it for long. Upon the journey, the hero faces serious conflicts, usually involving death-defying obstacles (if not literal death, then the hero will experience a figurative death such as the loss of a job or a relationship). Having faced the edge of death, the hero returns with a secret or special gift. Gift in hand, our hero returns home to leave his/her mark on the culture.

Barack Obama as a 'hero'

A natural storyteller, Barack Obama recognized and harnessed this power throughout his career. Regardless of political leanings, nearly all observers were unanimous in acknowledging Obama's ability to deliver a speech and tell a story. Recognized as a world-class rhetorician, Obama was also able to capitalize upon classic storytelling principles that have been around for thousands of years and implanted in the human psyche.[77] Obama's entire campaign followed the hero's journey very closely. Born of humble origins, Obama went on to Harvard Law School and community organizer in Chicago, where he experienced a great deal of difficulty at first but learned the secrets to help people[78]. Taking what he learned, Obama articulated his passion[79] and brought these secrets of hope and change to bear on the American culture throughout his campaign. Obama's core audience fully subscribed to the story he told in part because it so closely paralleled what they were used to seeing in any good story. Hitting all of the key elements of effective storytelling, Obama was able to capitalize upon the power of story to reach your audience.

Story in our lives

Experts who study story point out that storytelling has a very special place in our culture.[80] Some of the main functions of story involve the following points:

1. Story is used for people and organizations to help explain our origins.
2. Story helps establish an identity myth for individuals and groups.
3. Story is a means to communicate traditions and taboos of a social group, whether it is for a family, a culture at large, or a political movement.
4. Story simplifies complex narratives and ideas so that people can more easily understand them.
5. Story illustrates the natural order, helping us identify our position within our group.
6. Stories convey a complex history in a shortened and powerful fashion helping the audience to remember better.
7. Stories communicate a society's 'truths' about moral and ethical positions and values.
8. Stories help show relationships to authority and how we should act within this structure.
9. Story describes appropriate expected behaviors and norms for people in a social group from which we can model behavior.
10. Stories define reward and specify the paths to damnation or salvation.

Given all of these benefits that can be gained from effective storytelling, it is no wonder that Barack Obama made such effective use of this technique. The question remains, what exactly are the classic storytelling principles and how did Obama use them? And, more importantly, how can you use them in advancing your brand? That is what the rest of this chapter will focus on.

The stories we tell ourselves

What needs to be remembered with storytelling is that your audience takes whatever story you are telling them and, without thinking, weave it into their own personal life narratives. How many times have you gone to a movie and become so enwrapped in it that you forgot all sense of time? On these occasions, have you ever found yourself identifying with one or more of the central characters of the story? If so, then you understand one of the key criterions that make storytelling so effective, the suspension of disbelief.

When we hear a good story, we tend to process it at a deeper, emotional level rather than a superficial rational level. We are willing to accept ideas, no matter how implausible, because they speak to us at a meaning rather than a literal sense. In essence, when you tell a story you are asking your audience to collude with you by saying, 'I don't expect what you tell me to be true, just tell me a truth instead.' It is this very notion of story used to tell truth that makes it so powerful.

Many people get confused on the distinction between truth and true. True represents factual statements and can be proven or disproven. 'I voted for a particular bill.' 'This shovel is made of aluminum and wood.' Whenever we hear facts and narrative our logical brain kicks in and starts dissecting whether what we are being told is true or not.

Truth is another matter entirely. Great stories convey truth. The facts of the story don't need to be true in order to do this. Truth is that universal message that your audience believes in. It is the main theme of your story. We may not believe that Little Red Riding Hood almost mistook a wolf for her grandmother, but most people believe in the truth of being wary when talking to strangers. The truth to any story is the meaning behind the story that helps us explain our lives.

Consumers are complicit in the lies that stories tell. In order to do have your audience truly buy into your story, they must believe in the essence (i.e., the truth) of what your

story is telling. Successful marketers aren't lying, but rather telling stories that consumers choose to believe.[81] Essentially, people use stories to help give meaning to our lives. A well-framed story that subscribes to our world views helps us relate on an emotional level to the storyteller while also shaping our internal dialogues.

> **We may not believe that Little Red Riding Hood almost mistook a wolf for her grandmother, but most people believe in the truth of being wary when talking to strangers. The truth to any story is the meaning behind the story that helps us explain our lives.**

Whereas most traditional advertising attempts to attach social meaning to products and services, the use of story and myth can be used to show people how to live meaningfully. The story itself becomes the meaning for the consumer in this model.[82] When successfully employed, storytelling taps into the personal stories we tell ourselves every day. We all cast ourselves in our own daily scenarios, and effective storytellers use this.

Barack Obama as a storyteller

This ability to convey his point by tapping into people's personal stories served Obama very well. Early in his campaign, Obama often found himself having to give pep talks to his staff. His motivational techniques consisted of using story and metaphor to show them his own commitment to the campaign.[83] In reality, Obama had always used storytelling skills to great effect. In fact, at one point after the publication of his first book he had entertained thoughts of becoming a professional writer.[84] Barack Obama learned early on to express himself in a way that attracted followers. As noted by one of his early supporters in his Illinois senate race *"...He is a very thoughtful human being in the way he articulates ideas and the way he thinks about the world. And the older I get, the more I realize it is not always what you say, but the way you say it."*[85]

Indeed, this is true for many professionals and small business people. Your audience will attribute meaning to whatever you say. When you use correct storytelling techniques in your marketing efforts, you will be rewarded with an audience that will listen to you at a deeper emotional level, rather than a surface intellectual one. Powerful stories and therefore brands must own a mental landscape that consumers want to live in.[86] When done successfully, you will own a space in your audience's mind that will be very hard for your competitors to challenge. Correct use of storytelling principles will help propel you to the top of your field by allowing your audience to use your brand to interpret meaning in their own lives.[87]

When successfully employed, storytelling taps into the personal stories we tell ourselves every day. We all cast ourselves in our own daily scenarios, and effective storytellers use this.

Good stories have good conflict

In order to accomplish this, you must first understand and then use classic storytelling structure whenever discussing your brand's narrative. Classical story structure reflects action in real life. This relationship allows the audience to better understand and relate to the story[88]. Several common elements exist when creating your brand story.[89] The first element of successful story is passion, which is the energy that makes you want to tell the story. It is an irresistible spark that compels you to share your story with the world.

However, passion also requires the successful use of a hero to convey the message of your story. The hero is the character who is the central focal point for the narration of the story. This hero doesn't need to be "heroic" but is better thought of as the protagonist. As we will see in the next chapter, there are many forms that your hero can take, all of which can be incredibly effective when properly deployed.

All good stories also require a problem or conflict in order to convey an eternal message. Therefore, all good stories always have an antagonist with which the hero finds his or her conflict. As we will see, successful brands are the most successful when they have an enemy to rail against. As Barack Obama correctly recognized, the enemy in your story doesn't have to be a person (e.g., George Bush), but can be a system (e.g., Big Government) or a prevalent thought (e.g., lack of insiders' understanding for the common man).

What separates a good story from a not so good story is the notion of awareness. This awareness is the inspiration that the hero has which motivates him or her to see the problem and fight for a solution. Last we have transformation as the last element of a well told story. Our heroes take action to change their world, and by doing so they change themselves and the world around them. By following this classic approach you will find a built-in acceptance for your story because people are pre-conditioned to receive stories in this manner. If you really wish to be successful though, you must also frame the story in terms that the audience understands. This will insinuate itself with their preconceived notions and reinforce any biases they are already feeling.[90] While politicians in general (and Obama in particular[91]) are often accused of pandering to the base, this is actually quite effective. The notion of preaching to the choir in the terms they best understand, combined with storytelling technique, is a powerful combination indeed.

> *As Barack Obama correctly recognized, the enemy in your story doesn't have to be a person (e.g., George Bush), but can be a system (e.g., Big Government) or a prevalent thought (e.g., lack of insiders' understanding for the common man).*

When building a brand there are many different forms of stories that can, and should be, told. Perhaps the most important story that an organization tells is its creation story.[92] It is human nature to wonder where we come from. Cultures do this with their myths. People do it when we ask our parents to tell us about what it was like when we were born. Organizations and brands do it by telling how they were created. Creation stories abound in business and politics. Who in business doesn't know of Steve Jobs, Bill Gates, or Phil Knight? The creations of Apple, Microsoft, and Nike have achieved almost mythic status.

Create your creation story

A creation story is essential for people's belief systems. Your audience won't believe in something that didn't start somewhere. People are always asking themselves the question "where's that from?" If you want your audience to believe in what you are doing, you have to answer this. Especially when first starting out as a relative unknown. While announcing his candidacy for the presidency, Barack Obama *"started out, as all good organizers do, by telling the story of why they were gathered there that day - first narrating his audience's story, then narrating his own."*[93] By explaining his origins and how he came to be, Obama was able to get his followers to form a belief system involving him. In fact, a good creation story is essential to the development of early supporters. Good stories in general and creation stories in particular, allow people to not only define themselves but transform themselves.[94] Essentially the stories that Obama told, especially the early ones to his earliest supporters, allowed his audience to believe better of them by buying into these stories.

Identify your organizational stories

These creation stories are the first of many organiza - tional stories that businesses and individual brands tell.[95] Through the use of narrative and story, organizational stories become part of the organizational culture, helping organizations convey their shared values.[96] People who become involved in an organization after its initial inception now have the tools to understand and convey what it is that the organization is all about, and more importantly, how it relates to their lives. The successful brand creates many different back stories for itself.[97] These back stories are the history behind a product or brand, and how they became what they are today. It has real characters and a believable tale that show how these characters have evolved to overcome challenges. Many different back stories can be employed, all of which could be successful if you use the correct technique and character development. Also, truly powerful stories are a call to action for the faithful. They express an urgency of events and circumstances that show the need for a timely, strategic response.[98] This sense of urgency was prevalent throughout the entire Obama campaign.[99] Barack Obama fostered the notion that he had to enter the presidential race even with very little governance experience because the needs of the country were so urgent. Combined with powerful storytelling techniques, Obama successfully gained the agreement of his core audience providing him with the foundation to spread his story even further.

The telling of your story allows you to take your message and deliver it with impact. The most powerful storytelling allows you to conceptualize and communicate your message to your audience, convincing them in the process.[100] Simply put, most thought takes place at the unconscious level and effective story communicates at this level. It is imperative that a brand recognize how to appeal to this emotional aspect of people as well as the logical. This has been proven in many studies where narrative ads were shown to be more appealing than factual ads as well as causing higher levels of message involvement for the consumer.[101] Recognizing this, Barack Obama aired commercial ads that focused on a narrative appeal to his audience, rather than a logical one. The best example of this is perhaps the 30-minute infomercial he aired during the latter portion of the general election entitled "American Stories, American Solutions."[102] In it Obama tells many "American stories" of people he encountered throughout the campaign and what his plans for the country were. The infomercial played to reinforce Obama's message to his supporters and to introduce it to those who (by some major fluke) had not heard of it.

With this 30 minute commercial, Barack Obama showed that he fully understood another critical aspect to effective storytelling; the correct framing of your story. To be effective, a good story must not only follow the structure previously discussed, but it must also play to the cultural context in which it is being told.[103] *Business and politics do NOT take place external to our culture.* Rather, a business cannot operate within a culture without being part of that culture's history, traditional culture, and society. If you can associate your business story to popular culture or stories that already resonate with your target audience, then you are much more likely to experience success. Because this idea is so incredibly important and powerful we will discuss it in much more detail later.

> **Business and politics do NOT take place external to our culture. Barack Obama fostered the notion that he had to enter the presidential race even with very little governance experience because the needs of the country were so urgent. Combined with powerful storytelling techniques, Obama successfully gained the agreement of his core audience providing him with the foundation to spread his story even further.**

Marketing implications of this chapter:

- There are several necessary requirements for successful story marketing. Heed these and take your brand to the next level:

  - Find an audience that already has the worldview you are trying to sell. It is much easier to convince people to believe in something they already believe in!

  - People will make quick, permanent decisions based on first impressions. Your creation story has to grab them and hold them.

- Good marketers tell stories that people believe. While your story doesn't necessarily have to be true to have impact, it MUST convey some TRUTH, or message that your audience believes in.

- Your story should be seen as being authentic. Again, this doesn't mean it has to be 100% true, but it should show that you fully understand the language and thoughts of your audience and tell your story in their language.

- There are five key principles to employ when creating great stories for your brand:

  - Your story should immediately engage your audience; drawing them into belief and action.

  - Truly great stories don't appeal to our logic, but rather our emotions.

  - Your story (especially at first) doesn't have to appeal to everyone. Actually, you are often better served by targeting your story to the insiders of your target audience

  - Don't be afraid to talk the language of your audience and reinforce their preconceived notions. In fact, this should be encouraged.

  - Ideally, you want your audience to spread your story for you, not just be a core group of people listening to your story. Good stories are the ones that involve your audience by allowing supporters to take your story and modify and spread it in their own ways. The dissemination of Barack Obama's story was essential to the campaign.

- The most powerful stories are the ones that already agree with your audience's world views.

- Stick to basic plot points and story structure when creating your story. People are used to seeing plots in specific patterns and genres, and you don't want to deviate too far from what has already been established over thousands of years (after all; how many Boy Meet Girl movies have you seen?).

- Remember that you're telling a story. Good stories entertain and great stories reveal truth about your customers and their circumstances.

- Keep your story consistent. Good stories are simple and don't involve contradictory elements.

- The development of a great character is essential to your story. Be sure to show your character as the hero in the hero's journey.

- Brands are statements of values, so you need to be sure to project values within your story; especially the truth that your audience subscribes to.

- Make sure that your story is entertaining to its audience. Frankly, if your story is boring or doesn't follow expected convention then your audience is likely to tune you out.

- Remember that conflict is central to any good story. When telling a brand story, though, be sure that the conflict is controlled, so that you can properly point out who the enemies are and how you plan to overcome them. Show your audience that you hold the secret to dealing with the inherent conflict!

- And, if you haven't already, be sure to write your creation story! This is what will set the tone for who you are, what you believe, and what you will do for your audience.

CHAPTER 10

Who are you? Finding your voice

"What Washington needs is adult supervision."

BARACK OBAMA, fundraising letter, Oct. 2006[104]

As mentioned in the previous chapter a crucial step to understanding your role in the minds of your audience is to cast what you do in storytelling principles. Central to this is the idea of character. Your true role is the character you adopt in all of your marketing efforts. It is how your audience sees you. Successful marketers create an attractive character that resonates with their audience. This is what Barack Obama did. This is what you can do as well.

When you tell your story you must always be thinking in terms of your hero. The hero in your story is your central character. Heroes take many forms but all have something in common; people recognize the character's persona and can instantly understand it (although they don't necessarily identify with it). There are many classic characters that have withstood the test of time. These characters are timeless and universal.[105] All cultures, to greater or lesser degrees, have discovered and used these characters in their stories for generations as have successful writers and other storytellers.

Timeless and universal characters

These characters, or archetypes, have easily identified traits and habits that allow the audience to quickly classify them.[106] This commonality is what makes the use of archetypes so powerful. In simplest terms an archetype is a stereotypical representation of something. It is what provides the mental shorthand we need to quickly classify without having to spend too much mental energy doing so. There are several different archetypes that we have grown accustomed to seeing, and when you cast yourself in one of these roles your audience will immediately start ascribing the archetype's characteristics to you.

For example, you might cast yourself as a hero who takes on challenges and improves yourself in the process. You might be seen as the all-wise and knowing sage who understands the world at a deeper level than others. You might be a regular person, just looking to do your job and fit in. You could even go so far as to cast yourself as a rebel who wants to shake up the system and bring about change. While not all researchers agree on the number of classic characters (estimates range from 12 to 45[107]), it is generally agreed that there are a finite number and that they are all readily identifiable to your audience.[108]

Knowingly or not, Barack Obama cast himself in the role of a "ruler." Ruler characters seek control.[109] Rulers want to avoid chaos by taking control. Their intent is to create a prosperous, successful community through leadership. While others might assume that others will protect them, the ruler does not. It is important for a ruler to be in control of all aspects of his or her life. Therefore, the first tendency of a ruler character is to be in charge and lead others to create the environment that the ruler envisions. Rulers do not want to be told what to do, but modern rulers need to appear that they are building consensus because most consumers don't like to be told what to do either. The basic philosophy of a ruler is that if you lead in a way to enhance other people's lives, then they will reward you with their loyalty.

> *Seeing Barack Obama as a cool, unflustered leader let in great part to his 'rock-star' appeal with several reported instances of event organizers booking Barack Obama for rallies rather than rock groups because he would sell more tickets.*

Ruler characters appear especially appealing during turbulent times.[110] Many people, seeking a sense of order in their lives, will gravitate towards a ruler character as someone who can and will take charge and lead them to better times. Recognizing this, Barack Obama was able to convince his followers that he was the "adult" that Washington needed to get things working again. He positioned himself as someone outside of Washington politics who understood the needs of his audience and could lead the change that his audience sought.[111]   Obama was quick to point out the generational difference between himself and the Clintons. He used this to reinforce the notion that he was the fresh outsider who could change Washington politics.[112] Often discussed throughout the campaign was Obama's "coolness."[113] The idea that he was above petty squabbling and getting ruffled only served to reinforce his ruler credentials with his audience.   In fact, Obama being seen as the cool, unflustered, leader led in great part to his "rock-star" appeal with several reported instances of event organizers booking Barack Obama for rallies rather than rock groups because he would sell more tickets.[114] Being apart from the crowd made him almost more desirable to his audience and many of his supporters almost regarded him as royalty, replete with people being known to faint at his rallies.[115]

> *If you want to create a truly powerful character that resonates with your audience, you must learn to talk the talk and walk the walk. People will spot you for a fraud unless you truly understand your audience and think like one of them. Once you've done this though, you have gone a long way in terms of establishing your identity in the mind of your audience.*

While creating a ruler character was very effective for Barack Obama, there are many other roles that you can choose when creating your character. The key to any of these roles is to understand the motives driving the character as well as your audience. Your chosen role does not have to be the same as your audiences but it does need to be complementary to your audience's desires and how they see themselves. Hence Obama could cast himself as a ruler, while obviously the greatest majority of his followers were —— followers. In order to win the hearts and minds of your audience, it is important that you become an insider into the way they think.[116] You must learn to talk the talk and walk the walk. People will spot you for a fraud unless you truly understand your audience and think like one of them. Once you've done this though, you have gone a long way in terms of establishing your identity in the mind of your audience.

Creating a role; defining your attractive character

The good news is that you can create your role from scratch. In fact, you have a distinct advantage if you start as an unknown in the market when establishing your role. Being new is often a good thing in the eyes of your audience.[117] People are drawn to the word "new." By casting himself as a new form of politician, Barack Obama was able to take advantage of this simple principle. In this case, not being well-known on the national scene worked to his distinct advantage. Before beginning his presidential quest, Obama turned to Tom Daschle. Daschle, among others, helped urge Obama to run for the presidency because he had at least three strengths: 1) His newness in Washington; 2) His national fame; 3) His natural gravitas. Daschle argued that it was better to run as an unknown without a record so that he could more easily attack the Washington establishment.[118] Essentially, what Obama realized was that he was a blank slate candidate who could therefore become whatever he needed to be for his audience. Summing this philosophy quite nicely, Obama wrote, *"I am new enough on the national political scene that I serve as a blank screen on which people of vastly different political stripes project their own view."*[119] When done properly you too can mold your character to fit what your audience desires.

> *If you're starting from scratch, you actually have an advantage over your competition. Now is the time to create your attractive character in the fashion you desire. When done properly you can mold your character to fit what your audience desires.*

However, being a blank slate is not nearly enough. Your "new" brand must have a name and a voice. Barack Obama actually had a couple of advantages prior to entering the race that while on the surface may seem to have worked against him were, in reality, beneficial. First, his name.

While Obama would joke about his being "a tall, skinny guy with big ears and a funny name,"[120] from a marketer's perspective this actually stood to his advantage. Many times being different is good for a brand. *People are hardwired to detect irregular things, so something like a unique name can make you stand out from your competition and gets you noticed.*[121] In addition, one of the keys to Barack Obama's early success was his garnering the support of the younger voter. While in the past brand names were often created to inspire confidence and stability, the trend in recent years has been to create newer, hipper names.[122] This is especially prevalent for younger people, who are more drawn to brand names that appear cutting-edge and looking for brands that connect with them on a more personal level.

So, a good name is the first step to building what in marketing would be considered an attractive character. However, even if your name isn't necessarily unique, you can still follow the remaining steps to building an attractive character that resonates with your audience. In marketing, perhaps the most important thing you can do to create a role for yourself and your brand is to establish yourself as a market maven.

Basically, a market maven is a person who all others in an industry turn to for advice and guidance. This is the person (or brand) that sets the standards for your particular niche. Carefully crafting your market maven position makes you the automatic expert in whatever you do and most people will naturally gravitate to you over your competitors. After all, you are the leader in your particular niche!

There is a truism in marketing that, all things being equal; your audience will embrace the first brand that establishes its position in a particular category.[123] After all, if you are the first then you must be the leader and know more about that particular category than your competition. Even if everyone does things the same way, the person or organization that expresses what you do to your audience first will usually win. This is the notion of pre-emptive marketing. Once you say it, you own it. If no one else in your industry was clever enough to say it to your audience first, well, too bad for them.

As discussed, a key for marketers is to uniquely position their brands in the minds of their audience. When your audience thinks of the product/service you offer, you want to be the first one that comes to their mind. Essentially, creating your market maven position sets you apart from your competition by positioning yourself as the "originator" of an idea or approach, and by extension, the best and most competent at using it.

Smart marketers know and use this approach regularly. Barack Obama did. You can as well.

> **There is a truism in marketing that, all things being equal; your audience will embrace the first brand that established its position in a particular category. Even if everyone does business the same way, once you say it you own it. If no one else in your industry was clever enough to say it to your audience first, well, too bad for them.**

Discovering your marketing persona

The first step in establishing yourself as a market maven is creating your attractive character. This is where you will tell your audience who you are. What is your background? What are your interests? What are your motivations? Essentially, you are building rapport with your audience by identifying the role you wish to play with them and telling your story. Does your role suggest that you have always taken care of others and made the world a better place? Then perhaps your role is a caregiver. Have you always sought ways to express yourself and your creativity; leaving your mark on the world? Then your role could easily be a creator. As mentioned, there are many different roles that you can adopt. The key is to be sure that your chosen role is one that resonates with your audience and that allows you to express the motivations of yourself and your audience.

> *The process of writing his first book allowed Barack Obama to identify and convey his personality. The very fact of putting your memoir out to your audience says, 'this is what I want you to know about me and I don't mind being public about it.' It established your leadership credentials by this fact alone.*

This is essentially what Barack Obama did when he wrote his first book, <u>Dreams From My Father: A Story of Race and Inheritance</u>.[124] The entire book discusses Obama's searching for his identity. It lays the foundation for how he thinks and what led him to that point in his life. His story is one that appeals to the searcher in all of us. Everyone struggles with their identity, so through this book Obama was able to tell us who he is while tapping into the yearning we all have to better know ourselves. It is known that in order to attract passionate consumers, powerful brands must evoke a dynamic personality.[125] The process of writing his first book allowed Barack Obama to identify and convey his personality. The very fact of putting your memoir out to your audience says "this is what I want you to know about me and I don't mind being public about it." It establishes your leadership credentials by this fact alone.

However, if Obama would have stopped after this book, he could have had a successful writing career but his election to the Presidency of the United States would have been more doubtful. And this is because, knowingly or not, Barack Obama made a crucial choice that served him immeasurably well in the election; he wrote his manifesto.

A manifesto is, quite simply, a public declaration of your opinions. This is exactly what Barack Obama did when he wrote his second book; <u>The Audacity of Hope</u>.[126] In this book Obama expresses his thoughts on what should be a new type of politics and tells his story establishing his credibility in implementing his suggestions. There are several steps to writing an effective marketing manifesto and most people (politicians included) get it wrong. Obama got it right.

Writing your marketing manifesto

The first step to writing a proper marketing manifesto is to thoroughly understand your target audience. You have to identify their anxieties. What are the biggest problems that your audience faces? What are the inherent problems in the market? At this point it is essential to thoroughly understand your audience as discussed previously. When Barack Obama did community organizing, he was actually conducting thorough market research into the problems and motives of his core target audience.

As Obama discovered when he was talking to community leaders and members, people usually will tell you the symptoms of the problem, not the problem itself. At this stage of the process, it is crucial that you talk and listen to your audience, with an emphasis on listening. As Obama correctly noted in <u>The Audacity of Hope</u> while discussing his early campaigning days, *"… whether I was meeting with two people or fifty, whether I was in one of the well-shaded, stately homes of the North Shore, a walk-up apartment on the West Side, or a farmhouse outside Bloomington, whether people were friendly, indifferent, or occasionally hostile, I tried my best to keep my mouth shut and hear what they had to say."* [127] By truly listening to your core audience, you will begin to uncover the problems that they face and the type of solutions that they seek.

It is crucial though that you don't stop at the surface problem, but dig deeper with your audience to discover the underlying problem that leads to the surface problems. At this step, you actually want to point out all of the surface problems that your audience is facing and how much they are impacted by them. Now is when you start listing the many difficulties your audience encounters and point out how they are suffering from them. Barack Obama did this in <u>The Audacity of Hope</u> where he pointed out problems with politics, faith, race relations, world relations, and family issues, among others.

What makes a marketing manifesto truly powerful is what you do once you've elicited all of the problems that your audience faces. This step entails you taking all of the surface problems and showing how they are, in fact, nothing more than symptoms of some larger problem that you've identified. Barack Obama was able to take surface problems such as unemployment, race relations, the war in Iraq and others and trace them back to the then current politicians and politics as usual. In this one bold move, Obama was able to tie all problems that voters were facing into the idea that "*...having the audacity to believe despite all the evidence to the contrary that we could restore a sense of community to a nation torn by conflict; the gall to believe that despite personal setbacks, the loss of a job or an illness in the family or a childhood mired in poverty, we had some control - and therefore responsibility - over our own fate.*"[128]

> **When Barack Obama subsumed all problems under the guide of 'Hope', 'Change', and 'Yes We Can' he essentially usurped all of his competitors who were merely talking about jobs and crime. After all, it was the entire mindset of the Washington establishment that needed to change, and if we didn't do that, then politics as usual would ensure that nothing else would truly change.**

With this one brilliant move, Obama was able to suggest to his core audience that the problems they thought they were having were actually merely subsets of a single, larger problem. Your core audience now feels even closer rapport with you because you have put in words what they have been feeling and couldn't quite express. Your core audience now experiences that "aha" moment that only you truly understand their problems. All other solutions to the surface problems are now merely band-aids and you are the real deal. Everyone else is merely talking about symptoms, while you're talking about SOLUTIONS! So, when Barack Obama subsumed all problems under the guise of "Hope", "Change", and "Yes we can" he essentially usurped all of his competitors who were merely talking about jobs and crime. After all, it was the entire mindset of the Washington establishment that needed to change, and if we didn't do that, then politics as usual would ensure that nothing else would truly change.

Now that your audience has had their "aha" moment, they start spreading your word for you. It is a human tendency for people to feel almost a sense of smugness when we feel that we alone have the right answer.[129] Because of this, your audience will feel a desire to share the "solution" with others, with the solution being you and your brand.[130] *If correctly done, you have now established yourself as the only one who truly understands the deeper problems and can therefore offer THE SOLUTION. Your audience will recognize this and help spread your message far and wide.*

Creating a role and offering a solution worked for Barack Obama. When done properly, you can make it work for you as well.

Marketing Implications of this chapter:

- The first step to successfully identify yourself to your audience is to thoroughly understand the needs and motives of your audience. What do they most want? What are they most bothered by? Understanding this is the first step to defining a leadership position in their minds.

- Realize that there are universal characters (archetypes) that have resonated with humanity for generations. These are the timeless characters that we all know and understand from story.

    - Rather than creating a brand new character, it is far easier and much more powerful to work with one of the existing characters that everyone is used to seeing.

- Remember that each universal character has its own unique motives and goals. By aligning your brand's personality with these motives and goals you will make yourself readily identifiable to your audience.

- Also remember that your chosen character has to complement the motives and goals of your audience as well. If someone is looking to be led, then lead them. If someone is looking to be taken care of, then take care of them. If someone wants to overcome obstacles, help them!

- Once you've identified the personality characteristics of your role, it is time to start telling your story. Begin to tell people who you are and what you stand for. Use the common story structure discussed previously.

- If you are marketing yourself, feel free to use your own name, even if it might be a little unusual. If you don't have an unusual name, that's okay too; your manifesto is far more important. If you are branding a product or service, same rule applies.

- As you begin to tell your story, create your manifesto. What do YOU stand for?

  - Identify all known problems and solutions that exist within your chosen market.

  - What do these known problems have in common? What is the subsuming problem?

  - Propose a solution for the overarching problem. You are now the one with the SOLUTION and all of your competitors are merely pretenders offering band-aid solutions.

- Keep your manifesto in alignment with your audience, your role, and your identified truths. Essential to this entire process is that you believe in the truth of what you are selling as discussed in previous chapters. If you don't believe in your solution, your audience won't either.

- Don't be afraid to put yourself out there. When done properly, your audience will love you for it. Become the spokesperson for your audience and they will reward you with their loyalty.

CHAPTER 11

The Art of the Conflict; or, Good Enemies Make Good Marketers

"We have been told we cannot do this by a chorus of cyn-ics who will only grow louder and more dissonant in the weeks to come. We've been asked to pause for a reality check. We've been warned against offering the people of this nation false hope. But in the unlikely story that is America, there has never been anything false about hope. For when we have faced down impossible odds; when we've been told that we're not ready, or that we shouldn't try, or that we can't, generations of Americans have responded with a simple creed that sums up the spirit of a people. Yes we can."

Barack Obama; Speech following
New Hampshire Primary January 8, 2008.

All good stories need an antagonist, a foil. When a story doesn't have conflict, it is just, well, boring! Storytellers have known this for generations. Barack Obama knew it as well. Good enemies make good marketers.

In order to a story to hold our attention, it must show the hero being challenged. The reasons for this are many. First, it just makes for a better and more compelling story.[131] People are hardwired to detect obstacles. A good obstacle makes us pay attention and gets our blood flowing. This is similar to the fight-or-flight syndrome.[132] We tend to not notice things when they are part of a familiar landscape, but put something out of the ordinary into our view and we immediately react at a deep and emotional level. This is what good conflict does.

Mostly though, good conflict in branding takes advantage of naturally occurring enemies. The important part to realize is that enemies don't have to be people. In fact, more compelling enemies are systems or structures that prevent your audience from obtaining their yearnings. As discussed in a previous chapter, your brand can help your audience fulfill personal stories, which they find themselves living.[133] Central to this fulfillment is successfully identifying the obstacle that your audience is facing.

Barack Obama mastered the art of conflict in his campaign. While it might be argued that all politicians use conflict in their campaigns, Obama was more subtle (and therefore more powerful) in his approach. In essence, how we understand and deal with conflict represents our core values. People make judgments based on their values all the time. Values can't be proved, only defended. When others agree with our values, providing them arguments with which to defend their values will make them loyal to your argument and brand.[134] Barack Obama understood the conflicts and values of his core audience and was able to get them to promote him by defending their own beliefs that he had tapped into.

> **Don't be afraid to have an opinion on things. You can't cater to everyone! Don't be afraid of polarizing your audience. This is actually a good thing.**

Identifying natural conflicts

There are several things we need to understand if we are going to use conflict in our branding efforts. First, it's not enough to merely stand FOR something; you must stand AGAINST something if you want your brand to have true resonance with your audience. One of the reasons Apple Computer was able to take on entrenched Microsoft and IBM was that their core story was standing against corporate complacency. Nike became a powerhouse brand not just because of their running shoes, but because they stood against obstacles that prevent athletes from being their best. Barack Obama beat his Democratic rivals and later John McCain not so much because of what he was for, but what he was against (lack of optimism, government as usual, political in-fighting).

It's not enough to merely stand FOR something; you must stand AGAINST something if you want your brand to have true resonance with your audience.

This implies that the most important aspect for a would-be marketer to understand is the cultural context in which he or she is competing. No story takes place in a vacuum. You must have your finger on the pulse of the audience, not only what their hopes, fears, and desires are, but also on their environment. It is these contextual clues that will propel you forward to victory. When you understand the environment of your audience, you will be able to understand what it is that is really motivating them.

Second, you need to look at these cultural clues to determine where the naturally occurring conflicts are. It is true that all people in a culture tend to share common aspirations and ideologies. However, it is NOT true that all people in a culture share the attainment of these aspirations. In any given culture, at any given time, there will be people who are obtaining the dream and those who are not. This doesn't mean that those not obtaining the dream don't want it though. Far from it. These people are the ones who see the obstacles in their way and feel a deeper emotional commitment to obtaining the "dream."

Barack Obama recognized this simple, yet powerful, idea early in his political career.[135] All of the branding in the world won't make a lot of sense if you are not aware of the cultural context within which you are doing the branding. It is very important for the marketer to be aware of what is happening in his or her world, and how to react to the events of the day.

Because members of the same culture share the same ideologies, it is crucial for the successful marketer to look at where some members of the culture are being prevented from obtaining the culture's ideology.[136] Basically this says; look at what people in your audience think they should have and what they actually do have. If your audience believes that it should have full equality, but they don't feel that they do have full equality, you have a natural conflict to exploit. If your audience believes that government should represent them, but don't think that their government is representing them; you have a natural conflict to exploit. If your audience believes that hard work should be rewarded, but their hard work is not being rewarded; well, you get the idea.

Natural conflict is the most powerful

When your audience senses this natural conflict in their lives, human nature dictates that they try to rectify it.[137] People don't like dissonance in their thoughts and action. We like our thoughts and actions to be in mental alignment. The more powerful the dissonance is, the more compelled we become to try to solve it. For the marketer, this translates to people buying a brand not so much for what the brand actually does, but rather for how the brand helps the audience reconcile their conflicting thoughts and emotions. This is the housewife and mother who takes care of the family all day but has a glass of wine at night to remind her that she is more than just a caretaker. This is the CPA who has to follow rules all day long so on the weekend he rides his Harley to remind himself that it's okay to be a little bad sometimes. This is the young and idealistic voter who believes that politicians should listen to the will of the people and that Washington should not be the same 'ole, same 'ole, so they vote for Barack Obama because they have the right to some optimism.

So, this suggests that you need to understand your audience's wishes and desires as well as their value systems. Appealing to your audience's fantasies and wishes is an extremely powerful motivator. When you introduce your brand as the solution to an inherent conflict they are feeling, you can get your audience to appraise your brand in connection with the conflict. The emotional responses from the appraisal can then lead them to believe that your brand will help them reconcile their internal conflict.[138] Once your audience believes that your brand is the tool they need to reconcile these deep emotional divides, then you will be very successful indeed.

Mindsets are more powerful enemies than people

Barack Obama mastered another aspect of conflict creation. While many politicians attempt to sow discontent amongst the voters and position themselves as the solution, Obama railed against systems (and of course George W. Bush) that his audience believed were responsible for their unhappiness. Truly strong brands actually lead culture rather than following culture. This is accomplished by taking a provocative stand against the status quo, which is being seen as the contradiction of ideologies. In fact it has been argued that a truly strong brand will not really become powerful unless and until it alienates people who hold contradicting viewpoints. This is imperative to understand especially in the realm of politics, where it is true that powerful enemies make for better fans.[139] For example, Hurricane Katrina provided Obama with the context he needed to become a national voice. He left New Orleans knowing that as the only African American senator in the capital he was uniquely placed to give voice to the evacuees.[140] His early talks tackled issues such as Katrina and the war in Iraq as policy that was hindering his audience from obtaining their desires. You couldn't find a much bigger opponent than the entire United States Government and Obama used this to his advantage.

While later in his campaign Obama would name names and place blame on individuals, this came after he was well on his way to marketplace dominance

While Obama, like all of the Democratic contenders, did paint George W. Bush as the primary culprit of the nation's problems, he didn't stop there. Early in his presidential bid, Obama attacked divisive politics and the Washington system at large. His manifesto, <u>The Audacity of Hope</u>, was more of an attack on a system rather than individuals.[141] Initially positioning himself as above personal politics but rather attacking the status quo of politics was instrumental to his early success.[142] Once Obama was able to get his early supporters (mostly the young and/or idealistic) to believe that he was offering them a solution to an ideological divide (rather than an individual one) he was off to the races. Of course, while later he would name names and place blame on individuals, this came after he was well on his way to marketplace dominance.

Barack Obama was able to create discontent among Democrats towards Hillary Clinton by following these principles. While Clinton could be thought of as the known and trusted brand early in the primaries, Obama was able to wean support away from her by suggesting almost a violation of trust from her to many Democratic supporters.[143] Obama was able to paint Clinton and the Clinton machine as the epitome of Washington insiders and suggest that Washington as usual had to be revamped.[144] Because his early supporters believed in harmony and working together,[145] and that Washington was broken and preventing them from doing this, Obama's message served to set him apart in their minds. Translation: Hillary Clinton (and later John McCain) is part of the problem. Don't buy them, buy me.

Obama understood our current culture

This process worked especially well for Barack Obama given the current cultural context within which he was operating. Our current culture suggests that a majority of our culturally transmitted ideas come from our peers and not our history. This is especially prevalent in times of rapid change and technology advances. The result of this is that people often face uncertainty in their day-to-day life, especially with rapid change. When faced with fundamental uncertainties we tend to rely upon culturally transmitted myths to understand and live our lives.[146] Obama's supporters therefore felt an even stronger need to listen to each other and help spread the Obama message. Because his early supporters felt a great deal of emotional upheaval in their daily lives (i.e., they weren't getting what they thought society had promised them) and they were predisposed to help spread his message, Obama was able to catch and overtake Clinton rapidly.[147] Given these events, John McCain never had a chance.

Make an attitude your enemy and you will go far!

Last, as we know, the most successful brand stories encourage conflict. To be truly successful though you will want to take an extreme position initially and then gracefully move your story to the middle to appeal to the masses.[148] Your early supporters (the market innovators) will be drawn to your extreme position and help get the ball rolling because they are the most likely to feel the conflict you are discussing. The market majority though tends to be not quite as extreme as these insiders. They essentially want the light version of what you are selling so you need to encourage conflict, but perhaps not quite so dramatically, at this point. You could see this in action throughout Barack Obama's campaign as he started articulating more centrist viewpoints as the general election approached. While doing this though, you must retain fidelity with your core audience or they will most likely turn on you.

What are the hot buttons of the day? How can you use these when applying your evergreen story principles?

Marketing Implications of this chapter:

- Don't forget the principles of good storytelling. Contrasts are good. Point out the differences between you and your competitors.

- Don't be afraid to have an opinion on things either. You can't cater to everyone! Don't be afraid of polarizing your audience. This is actually a good thing.

- Always look for the inherent conflicts people are feeling in their daily lives. What do they expect that they feel prevented from getting? If you can tap into this anxiety, you are well on your way to identifying truly powerful conflicts.

- The most powerful conflicts you can employ are not against people, but against mindsets and attitudes. Apple Computer did not attack Microsoft as a company or individual, but as a mindset of corporate complacency and refusing to think creatively. Nike did not attack any person or company, but the mindset of not pushing yourself the hardest to excel. Barack Obama did not (at first) attack individuals, but the attitude of people being helpless to affect Washington politics. Make an attitude your enemy and you will go far!

- Many times it is beneficial for the marketer to not say what he or she is for, but rather what he or she is against. This will draw out your supporters much more effectively.

- Appeal to your audience's fantasies and wishes. If you can show your audience how what you're branding is a tool to their fulfillment, you will most likely garner their support.

- When you have properly identified a conflict and positioned your brand as a solution (i.e., tool) to resolving this conflict you can get your audience to help spread your message for you.

- If you are looking to oust an entrenched competitor, show your audience how your competitor has violated some form of trust with your audience. This will give you the opening you need to offer your solution.

- Once your brand has taken hold with your core audience, you now need to think of ways to tell your story to the masses.

- Don't change or quit your core story and con-flict; this will only serve to alienate your strongest supporters.

- Do think of ways to perhaps lighten up your message so that the middle market can accept it without losing your core audience.

- Do identify sub-markets within your audience that your larger market can relate to (although they may not necessarily be a part of). Once identified, you can use the sub-markets to help you in your branding to the larger market.

- Most importantly, always be a student of the culture you are selling to. The best branding strategies are contextually relevant. While the principles of market-ing and branding are fairly timeless, their success is greatly dependent on your environment. What are the hot buttons of the day? How can you use these when applying your evergreen story principles?

CHAPTER 12

Step 4: Aspiration Delivery

After you have identified the needs of your audience and the role you will fulfill for the audience, you need to deliver. In today's world of marketing, it's not enough to merely talk about what you do in terms of features and advantages; you must also deliver on people's aspirations!

The next step in the **BARACK Marketing System,** Aspiration Delivery, is one of the most important. If you don't learn to speak the language of your audience, then you will not be talking to them where it most matters, their emotions. People think in symbols and images. While we might like to pretend that we are wholly rational, smart marketers know that this is far from the truth. People buy on emotion and justify with reason. If you are not able to speak this emotional language your audience desires, then you will not be nearly as successful as those who do.

In today's society there really is nothing new under the sun. There are only so many lipsticks, fast food restaurants, financial planners, politicians, etc. to go around. Most people adopt a 'been-there-done-that' attitude when you try to bring something new to the market. After all, are you really that new and different? Probably not. And even if you were, does your audience actually believe it when they hear the words "better," "new and improved," "faster," and such not? Again, probably not. The simple truth today is that we all pretty much have everything we need from a practical perspective. Yet, practical seldom sells. If you want to really rise to the top of your field or industry you must learn the language of the intangible.

> *If you don't learn to speak the language of your audience, then you will not be talking to them where it most matters, their emotions.*

This begs the question. How does a new (or relatively unknown) brand capture the imagination and hearts of the market? What did Barack Obama do prior to and during his campaign to gain such loyal support, money and votes? He learned to speak the language of his audience. Barack Obama mastered the art of metaphor and emotion in his communications with his audience. He learned how to express himself so that people would buy into his messages at a deep, almost subconscious, level thus ensuring himself their attention and loyalty.

The good news is that there really is nothing magical about this. Successful marketers and copywriters have known (and used) these techniques for years. It's only a matter of pulling back the curtain and taking a look. So, ladies and gentlemen please take your seats and enjoy the show.

CHAPTER 13

Symbolic Meaning and Metaphor

"...Katrina was not the end of the tough times for New Orleans and you will continue to face your own tests and challenges in the years to come. But if someone were to ask me how the tree stands on this August day, I would tell them that the seeds have sprouted, the roots are strong, and I just saw more than 500 branches that are ready to grow again."

Barack Obama, August 11, 2006,
Xavier University Commencement Address.[149]

When Barack Obama offered his commencement address to Xavier University, he created a powerful connection with his audience both in attendance and elsewhere. It is not uncommon for a commencement address to contain inspiration and hope for the future. This is pretty much expected. Yet, what Obama was able to do quite successfully was to mix his message of hope with symbolism that resonated with his audience. By planting the mental image of his audience being the roots of a devastated tree, certain to sprout forth better and stronger than before, he invoked a powerful metaphor allowing his audience to visualize themselves in terms they had not previously been thinking. As any good marketer will do, Obama successfully employed emotional marketing through the use of symbolic meaning and metaphor.

Emotional marketing trumps rational marketing. As much as we'd like to believe so, most people do not think rationally. Over 80% of interpersonal communication is non-verbal and takes place at the metaphor level.[150] Therefore, most "thought" actually takes place at the subconscious level and many times people cannot even explain or understand why they think the way that they do. Words create pictures and images in the mind of your audience. The more symbolic and powerful your phrases are, the more likely your audience will be to think in terms of the imagery they represent, rather than the actual words. Powerful psychological and societal factors are at work whenever we think in metaphors. Metaphors are comprised of real things that people can relate to that have been artistically arranged to reveal hidden truths.[151] Metaphors resonate with people at a very deep level. Oftentimes, we can't even say for sure why we think or believe things. When asked to put into words, people fall short.

Metaphors and symbolic meaning

Metaphors are representations of one object or thought by another. They are non-literal expressions that allow us to make mental substitutions of what we know to something new. Metaphors allow people to look at things in different ways, and the successful marketer makes great use of this substitution habit.

This is because people don't think in words, but rather images. Symbolism rules the day. The internal images we all carry around in our minds will tell a more compelling story and have more meaning than anything any politician or marketer could ever say. Successful brands are not seen as commodities by their audience but are projected in emotions and inspiration.[152] This forges a deeper connection, and therefore more loyalty between the brand and its audience. Therefore, it is very important that if you want to be a successful marketer and propel yourself to the top of your field, you have to learn to talk the language of your audience. This language is metaphor and symbolism.

> *The often-used example is to think of an elephant. When asked to do this, you will naturally form an image of an elephant in your mind, not create a list of its features.*

Successful marketers have known this for some time. We don't think in words, we think in pictures and images. Metaphors and symbolic meaning allow us to understand our world at a deep and profound level. Most communication occurs at the nonverbal level. The actual words we use are not as important as the meaning and context behind them. In addition, people's thoughts occur as images. When we think, we don't think in words but in the pictures the words conjure. The often-used example is to think of an elephant. When asked to do this, you will naturally form an image of an elephant in your mind, not create a list of its features. If you are looking to appeal to your audience's thoughts, the easiest and best way to do this is through the use of metaphors. Metaphors allow us to understand new information by putting it into context of images and thoughts that we already have. Experience helps people adapt their thoughts. We work all of our experiences into what we know and imagine, and try to make reason out of them. When we don't have a model to follow (i.e., we are faced with a new experience) we need to make sense of it. People are meaning-seeking creatures. We need to have structure and meaning to all aspects of our life. If your audience doesn't see the inherent meaning in what you are saying, you are going to lose them. Metaphors allow your audience to attach meaning to new information by putting it in context of things they already know and understand.

Strong brands arise from strong identities.[153] These identities can take different forms, with two of the forms being brand as person and brand as symbol (both of which Barack Obama successfully developed). The execution of the brand identity is created through symbols and metaphors, with a great deal of testing to determine those elements that have the most meaning to the consumer.

Barack Obama's use of imagery and symbolism

Barack Obama successfully spoke the language of metaphor and imagery. His speeches and writings painted word pictures in the minds of his audience, allowing them to form their own associations of Obama with a "new" kind of politician. Obama learned his distinctive voice early in his career while creating his writings. In his first book, <u>Dreams From My Father</u>, Obama learned to use metaphor and imagery to great effect.[154] Throughout his political career, Obama mastered the art of using symbolism in his speaking. Obama recognized the power of symbolism throughout his writings and campaign. In <u>The Audacity of Hope</u> he explained, *"The answer I settle on — which is by no means original to me — requires a shift in metaphors, one that sees our democracy not as a house to be built, but as a conversation to be had."*[155] Because metaphors are comprised of real things that people can relate to that have been artistically arranged to reveal hidden truths,[156] the proper use of metaphor allows marketers to frame the discussion they have with their audience as well.

Throughout his campaign, Barack Obama used words and symbols that allowed his audience to build emotional associations of being part of something historic. All of his actions seemed almost larger than life, letting his fans feel that they were partaking of something bigger and better. His creation of emotional, symbolic triggers such as the forum he chose to accept the Democratic Party nomination allowed his audience to believe that they too were involved in something bigger than themselves.

Obama announced his presidential campaign in Springfield, Illinois in the shadow of the Old State Capital. Several times throughout his speech he invoked the image of Abraham Lincoln presuming that he was an historic figure like Lincoln. Obama uses imagery and metaphor throughout the speech, as evidenced towards the closing passage:

"...the life of a tall, gangly, self-made Springfield lawyer tells us that a different future is possible. He tells us that there is power in words. He tells us that there is power in conviction. That beneath all the differences of race and region, faith and station, we are one people. He tells us that there is power in hope. As Lincoln organized the forces arrayed against slavery, he was heard to say: "Of strange, discordant, and even hostile elements, we gathered from the four winds, and formed and fought to battle through." That is our purpose here today. That's why I'm in this race. Not just to hold an office, but to gather with you to transform a nation.[157]"

The set used to deliver his acceptance speech at the Democratic Convention was both mocked and cheered, depending on the source, yet few could argue the emotional resonance that such a set conveyed. Consisting of columns that resembled a miniature Greek temple, the stage was similar in structure to those used in rock concerts. The podium was actually on a platform that rose from beneath the floor, thereby elevating him above the stage and the crowds. The venue itself broke from tradition of a nominee accepting the party's nomination at the convention site and instead was held on the 50-yard line of a football stadium, with 80,000 people in attendance (in addition to the millions watching on television). *When Obama spoke confetti rained down on him and fireworks lit the sky from locations around the stadium wall.*[158] *All in all, a very powerful symbolic display designed to show Obama as both presidential and invite the audience to believe that they were part of this magic.* In addition to Abraham Lincoln, Barack Obama would often compare himself to John F. Kennedy as well[159], helping to strengthen a key metaphor for his core audience.

Symbolic representation and your audience

Symbolic representation allows the marketer or politician to create word images in the minds of his/her audience. People do not generally think in terms of words, but rather pictures. By understanding the symbolic nature of what people are thinking, you can more closely align your product or service to the mental images that your audience already has. When incorporating new information into an existing knowledge structure, people will look for mental shortcuts to make the job of thinking easier. Complete comprehension of a new idea requires your audience to integrate the new idea with existing information. For example, think of what an animal on a newly discovered planet might look like. Chances are very good that your mental image of this animal will include such obvious features as ways to move (e.g., arms and legs) as well as eat and see (e.g., mouths and eyes). However, we are basing our mental images of this strange animal solely upon our experiences with animals here on earth. Because we can't even begin to comprehend what an animal we have never seen before would look like, we take the shortcut method of basing our images on what we already know.

It is this symbolic representation of new information that was so powerful for the Obama campaign, and is one that any successful marketer can take advantage of. Nonverbal communication is at the heart of most of our thinking. Through the effective use of metaphor and symbolism, Obama was able to reveal the hidden "truth" that his audience required. Metaphors allow the marketer to represent those things that people know, but often can't quite express in words. The use of the image-laden metaphor allows your audience to understand your message on a deeper, more visceral level.

> **People do not generally think in terms of words, but rather pictures. Through the effective use of metaphor and symbolism, Obama was able to reveal the hidden "truth" that his audience required.**

Barack Obama mastered the use of story and in fact positioned his entire campaign to appear almost as a mythological journey. Whereas most traditional advertising attempts to attach social meaning to products and services, the use of story and myth can be used to show people how to live meaningfully. The story itself becomes the meaning for the consumer in this mode.[160] Through correct use of mythological structure combined with powerful metaphor and symbolism, Obama was able to provide his audiences with much more than just a political candidate. He was able to provide his core constituency with a deep, emotional connection of Obama being the only candidate able to help them live out their own symbolic lives.

Using symbolism in your marketing

The nature of thought is a combination of conscious and unconscious actions.[161] The effective use of metaphor and story will appeal to people at an unconscious level, which will make them more likely to understand and agree with what is being said. The successful marketer understands that:

1. Most of the communication consumers engage in is nonverbal;
2. People's thoughts occur as images. Therefore the best way to approach these thoughts is through the use of metaphor;
3. Thoughts are based in experience, and that;
4. Reason, experience and emotion are all comingled in the mind of the consumer.

In essence, the correct use of symbolism allows the marketer to speak directly to the habitual mind of the audience. People make decisions with executive (i.e., rational) and habitual (i.e., emotional) minds.[162] The executive mind causes people to consciously focus on one thing at a time whereas the habitual mind allows us to bypass this mental energy by relying upon previously learned heuristics.

By simplifying the election to "Change" and "Yes We Can" Barack Obama allowed people to interpret his ideas more easily and therefore associate positive feelings to his campaign.

Barack Obama correctly understood that most thought takes place at the unconscious level.[163] Therefore it was imperative for his campaign to recognize how to appeal to the emotional aspect of people as well as the logical. Because the nature of thought is a combination of conscious and unconscious actions, the effective use of metaphor and story appeals to people at an unconscious level, which will make them more likely to understand and agree with what is being said.[164] Obama used a combination of techniques to bypass the rational filters of thought and appeal directly to emotion. For example, simple words and ideas lead to people feeling more positive about your brand.[165] His strategy of simplifying the election to "Change" and "Yes We Can" allowed people to interpret his ideas more easily and therefore associate positive feelings to his campaign.

The Obama campaign also mastered the art of the campaign rally. Successful marketers know that a highly emotional resonant moment will leave a lasting imprint on a person's mind.[166] It was not unusual for Obama's team to orchestrate rallies numbering in the tens of thousands and create backdrops reminiscent of Hollywood sets.[167] The careful orchestration of crowds and stage helped create very emotional moments for the participants thus guaranteeing a lasting impression. Not only did these rallies create lasting impressions, but they helped create strong loyalty from the attendees to Barack Obama by combining a highly emotional experience with the audience's sense of trust in Obama.[168]

Symbolism as emotional fulfillment

Barack Obama also used two other very effective techniques from his emotional marketing arsenal: providing his audience with fantasy fulfillment and preying on their fears. Appealing to your audience's fantasies and wishes is an exceptionally powerful motivator.[169] Understanding and talking to your audience's deepest psychological yearnings will motivate them at a very deep and personal level. Obama was able to position himself as the politician with the ability to bring "adult supervision" to Washington (at least in the eyes of his supporters). This is something that his supporters were long-ing for.[170]   Because a majority of his appeal was towards younger voters, there was a great sense of optimism and ide-alism in his campaign, pointed directly at this yearning his voters shared.

> **Arousing strong negative emotions and then offering a solution is a classic technique intelligent marketers (including Obama) have employed for some time. Why? Because it works.**

This fantasy fulfillment was counter-balanced by preying on the fears of many voters. Preying on fears can also be a very powerful emotion-generating technique. The key here is to offer hope as well. A very successful strategy is to threaten what people hold dear and then offer solutions.[171]   Obama successfully explored the fears that many Americans have (e.g., job loss, the ability to provide for self and family, race relations, war, etc.) and offered himself as the hope that they needed to survive the turmoil. Arousing strong negative emo-tions and then offering a solution is a classic technique intelli-gent marketers (including Obama) have employed for some time. Why? Because it works.

Last, Barack Obama and his campaign staff perfected the art of iconography. Icons are visual symbols that we use as mental shorthand. Many of them are based on universal themes that convey a message or emotion at a glance. For example, apples are commonly associated with both knowl-edge and the forbidden fruit. Sunrises are associated with a new day and new beginning. Icons tell stories without words. The famous sun -rising logo of the Obama campaign allowed the audience to interpret the message without the need for words.[172] This is especially powerful when your icon becomes synonymous with your brand. When our audience knows our brand story we don't need to constantly tell it to them, just remind them of it. Icons do this.

Marketing implications of this chapter:

- Remember that people process information both at rational and emotional levels, but that over 80% of our communication actually takes place at the non-verbal and emotional level. Therefore, it would greatly benefit you to be able to "talk" this language.

- A large portion of our non-verbal communication is symbolically based. People have an innate need to interpret our environment and often think in pictures and symbols.

- Creating apt metaphors for what your brand is about makes it easier for your audience to understand, and buy in to, what you are offering.

- Set the stage for your communications with your audience. The more you can incorporate symbolism (both through words and images) into your communications, the more successful you will be.

- Understand the deep yearnings that your audience has. By simultaneously making them fearful and positioning yourself as the solution, you will gain their commitment.

- When creating the symbols for your marketing efforts (both words and pictures) remember that simple phrases and images often convey more power than complex ones.

- Above all, if you can help your audience to believe that they are living out their symbolic lives through your brand, then you will have incredible support and loyalty.

CHAPTER 14

There is nothing new under the sun: Basic copywriting and advertising principles

"...I will say this, that I am suspicious of hype. The fact that I've become, that my 15 minutes of fame has extended a little longer than 15 minutes I think is somewhat surprising to me and completely baffling to my wife..."

Barack Obama, Press Conference Manchester NH, Dec. 10, 2006; after a book signing[173]

Principles of persuasion have existed for centuries. People are born with natural ability to persuade others. Every time a baby cries for food or a change, she is persuading her parents. If it weren't for persuasion, people would not get married or find employment. For approximately the last 100 years, persuasion has been scientifically studied and applied in the form of copywriting and advertising.[174]

Ask any successful copywriter about how to persuade people and they will tell you to appeal to the very basic emotions of fear and greed. These are followed closely by the favorites; pride, lust, and envy. Successful persuasion follows four rules of selling:

1. People don't like the idea of being sold.
2. While people don't like to be sold, they do like to buy.
3. People buy things for emotional reasons, not rational ones.
4. After they've been sold, people need to justify their emotional purchases with logical reasons.

A fundamental principle in all good advertising and copywriting is that people are selfish. Your audience doesn't care about you and your interests; they only care about their own self-interests.[175] Smart marketers recognize this fact and will always position their brand in terms of the audience's self-interest. Most politicians will say "give me your vote" without a good reason to do so. Most brands say "buy my product, give me the business you give to others" without giving the consumer a good reason why they should. Successful marketers will paint pictures in the mind of their audience to generate emotion about the brand. These marketers will make the audience feel good about the brand, not merely recite facts and statistics. The smart promoter creates verbal pictures that tease his audience's desires and cravings. You tempt your audience by appealing to their emotions. The ultimate goal of advertising is to motivate your audience to take action. People are motivated to act in their own self-interests by gaining positive feelings or reducing negative feelings.[176]

People persuade others in many different ways. Successful practitioners of persuasion realize that it begins with asking good questions, listening, and then appealing to the emotions of your audience.[177] Through this process the marketer understands what motivates his audience and is able to deliver accordingly. Barack Obama successfully understood his audience and gave them what they wanted to hear. He followed time-proven copywriting and advertising principles to accomplish this in his campaign literature and speeches.[178]

Like any good marketer, Barack Obama understood and expressed his audience's deep-seated hopes and fears; positioning himself as the solution to their pain.

Copywriting Principles

Good copywriting is very similar to good storytelling. To be a great marketer you must first master audience advocacy. This involves viewing yourself, your company, and your story through the eyes of your audience and having them feel that you are talking directly to and about them.[179]

Several thousand years ago, Aristotle was one of the first to point out the keys to good story structure. Classic story-telling structure applies to successful emotional branding and advertising. Aristotle showed three key elements of persuasion, which modern branders would be well-advised to learn. These three elements are: 1) credibility, 2) emotion, and 3) rationality. Using these elements successfully will allow users to suspend disbelief when listening to your advertising, and therefore become more willing accomplices to the story you are telling.[180] In fact, successful advertisers will tell you that, like Barack Obama in his speeches and advertising, powerful narrative will persuade more people than will factual advertising because the narrative ad is more likely to create emotional involvement.[181] Successful copywriters and advertisers are successful storytellers with a thorough understanding of some basic principles.

***Sound copywriting principles recognize several important facts*:**

- Most people are distrustful of advertising and don't believe hype. However, successful copywriters do need to provide abundant, specific evidence for their claims. The key is that you must present this evidence in a believable and credible manner.

- The real reason people buy is seldom the stated one.

- Most people don't want to do the work; they want the product to do the work for them.

- Many people are not even aware they have a problem until the copywriter points it out to them and then agitates them.

- People don't buy products for the actual product, but rather for the core value the product delivers.

- People like to feel good about the purchases they make, but don't want to feel that you are selling to them.

- There are different types of needs and motivations for people. Successful marketers identify the appropriate level of need and sell accordingly.

- Good copywriting does not express itself in boring language. The more emotive the language the better the word pictures. The better the word pictures, the more powerful the emotion. The more powerful the emotion, the more likelihood the marketer will sell her product and obtain the loyalty of her audience.

- Many people purchase products as props for their personal story fulfillment. If you can show how your brand/product is a tool for your audience's story, you will earn their hearts and their loyalty.

The Obama campaign applied most of these principles when promoting Obama by fully understanding the power of emotional advertising and branding.

Building rapport with your audience is a crucial first step to effective sales and copywriting.[182] To build rapport, you must show your audience that you absolutely identify with them and their situation. People buy from people they like. People buy from people like them. These are axioms in sales and copywriting that hold true for politics. Successful politicians need to appear that they are like the audience they represent. Barack Obama knew to always position everything he said in terms of the audience's self-interests. This is key to getting people to like you; you have to convince them that you understand their feelings and aspirations.

People buy from people they like and trust. Barack Obama convinced his audience that he truly understood their needs and wants, successfully creating stories that his audience bought into.

Understanding Your Audience

Understanding your audience is often easier said than done. Early in his career, Barack Obama mastered the art of probing his audience to determine their hopes and dreams.[183] Most copywriters have learned these techniques as well. You cannot sell to your audience until you understand them thoroughly.[184] Before putting pen to paper, good copywriters will determine what their audience fears more than anything. What do they desire more than anything? What are their hopes and aspirations? By asking and answering these questions, successful copywriters (and politicians) gain a thorough picture of their audience.

Getting Their Attention

Before your audience will consider what you have to say, you first need to get their attention. People need a reason for taking the time to listen to you. Headlines in copywriting fulfill this purpose, and every good copywriter knows that if your headline doesn't grab your audience, then they are not going to read anything else you have written. Similarly, in politics and speaking, you need some form of attention-grabbing headline. This could be the opening line of your speech, or something as simple as a slogan repeated through advertising.

In politics and business, you need some form of attention-grabbing headline. This could be the opening line of your speech, or something as simple as a slogan repeated through advertising.

Copywriting and advertising masters suggest the use of several guidelines when writing headlines and slogans.[185] These include:

1.   Be sure to get your audience's self-interest into every headline.

2.   If you have something new to show, be sure to get that in your headline/slogan.
3.   Combine curiosity with news to stimulate attention.
4.   Avoid negative and gloomy headlines/slogans. The positive approach will typically perform better.
5.   Suggest that there is a quick and easy way for your audience to get what they want.

Barack Obama was able to work in most of these guidelines through most of his speeches, ads, and other promotions.[186] Once he gained the attention of his audience, he was able to talk his audience's language to get them to listen to the rest of his message.

Talking Your Audience's Language

While many made arguments that Barack Obama did not represent most voters' interests, his key supporters would argue otherwise. He successfully built his brand by intensely focusing on the needs of his core constituents, allowing others to join the bandwagon later. A primary early market for Obama was the under-25 age voter. This audience prides itself on the ability to work with others and get along.[187] Coupling this with the natural tendency of many people to follow the herd[188], Obama was able to capitalize upon opinion-leaders to help spread his message. Later in his campaign, Obama had built enough critical mass to gain the support of people who might not have originally voted for him. Successful marketers know that people do not want to change their worldviews. We all have our biases in what we do.[189] Therefore, anything a marketer can do to help reinforce the biases of your audience, the more believable your story will be to them making you more successful. Barack Obama understood the biases of his core audience and the impact these people had on their followers. By playing to their pre-existing thoughts, he was able to harness their energy and support to his advantage. In addition, Obama learned a key rule that all successful copywriters know; you need to talk in specifics rather than generalities. When discussing his early community organizer days, Obama reflected that, "*The problem of gangs was too general to make an impression on people - issues had to be made concrete, specific, and winnable.*"[190] Successful marketers understand this as well and therefore make their copy points as specific as possible.

Also, people often like to follow the decisions and recommendations of others. By the latter phase of the Democratic primary campaign, Obama had built enough momentum from his core audience and opinion-leaders (such as journalists and newscasters) that many voters merely followed the herd. Once more, the Obama team showed a thorough application of copywriting and advertising principles. A strong tenet of copywriting is that you must provide ample evidence of the success of what you are selling. Because most of your audience doesn't have direct experience with your brand yet, they must rely on external evidence to justify purchasing your brand. Key endorsements and recommendations are a staple in copywriting. Look at any effective sales letter, and you will find it full of testimonials touting the success and value of the brand. Because such a large portion of the audience doesn't like to take risk, these testimonials serve to offer the support network and psychological well-being your audience requires to justify why they should buy something new. The Obama campaign was very successful at securing key endorsements that helped sway the less committed voter to consider, and ultimately vote, for him.[191]

When building rapport, you then create the hook of your offer. The hook is the self-interest laden benefit statement in your offer. When Obama spoke to audiences, he would always identify what it was that they wanted and provide it to them.[192] When marketers and copywriters create the hook, you have to analyze what it is that you audience wants above all else, and show them how they can get it by using your product.

Your offer must have a hook; the self-interest benefit laden part of your offer.

Wooing your audience

Another key principle to copywriting and sales is to ask for varying levels of commitment. Successful copywriters know that you have to build a case for whatever you're selling. If you jump into asking for a commitment too soon, you are likely to scare off your audience because they don't believe and trust you yet. Brands must first pass through the knowledge and commitment ascension ladder. Just as in courtship, you must start with listening to your audience and providing them with the basic knowledge they require before they can move to any type of commitment.

When asking for the commitment of a voter or consumer, the same principle applies. Wooing your audience, especially at the beginning of your relationship, is of utmost importance. Power questions and power statements are one key way to hook your audience from the beginning. Barack Obama used both power questions and statements during most of his speaking engagements. His speech at the 2004 Democratic Convention, widely credited for helping thrust him to the forefront of Democratic opinion leaders had many of these devices throughout.[193] Through the effective use of power statements your writing, advertising, and speaking appeals to the prejudices your audience holds, aligning your brand with their emotional state and beliefs. Provocative questions and stories will usually elicit an emotional response from your audience, especially if you are tapping into their existing belief structure. In turn, this heightened emotional state will make your audience more receptive to your message and to believing that your brand can offer the solution they seek.

A classic principle of copywriting is to take these emotions and then agitate them. It's not nearly enough to point out the problem that your audience is having; you have to show them all of the ways their lives are being impacted by not solving this problem. Once you have done this, you can then position your brand as the solution to these problems.

Producing an emotional response in your audience

Emotions sell. When people are emotionally invested in what you are saying, they will listen to you and take action. Therefore, the wise marketer needs an understanding of what emotions are and how to harness them in your advertising. Experts who study emotion suggest the following thoughts[194]:

- Emotions are about something. In order to fully understand a person's emotion, you must identify and analyze the object of their emotion to determine the attribute or characteristic that is responsible for the emotion.

- Emotions come from highly positive or negative appraisals. If something concerns us, we usually have a reflex emotion prior to our thinking about it.

- In order for an emotion to be motivating, we have to combine high arousal with a pleasant or unpleasant situation.

- Emotions make people want to act.

- Emotions are often expressed through involuntary body language. Experts at reading emotion rely on these cues to harness the emotion.

These principles of emotion lead to two very important points regarding emotional advertising:

1. If you feel that something is true, that is enough. Whether or not it is actually true doesn't matter and logic often won't hold any sway over you. Beliefs are truth.

2.   To generate an emotional response, project image over substance. The substance appeals to the logical/cognitive parts of our brains, but the imagery is a more direct route to our emotional behavior.[195]

The Obama campaign understood two key principles about emotional promotion: 1) Your audience's beliefs are their truth! And 2) Imagery is a more direct route to emotional behavior.

Preying on fears can also be a very powerful emotion-generating technique. The key here is to offer hope as well. A very successful strategy is to threaten what people hold dear and then offer solutions.[196] Barack Obama understood and applied this strategy in most of his speeches as well.[197]

Find your lead horse

Barack Obama was very successful at gaining core supporters early in his bid for the presidency.[198] In advertising, if you can get powerful testimonials and endorsements, the herd mentality kicks in for many people. This mentality suggests that many people are actually followers and will wait and see what others (especially key opinion-leaders) do before they decide on a course of action.[199] The Obama campaign was able to focus a great deal of their message on the early adopters and opinion leaders, who in turn were able to convince others. In fact, a great deal of modern advertising uses the principles of conformity to get your audience to try your brand.[200] Obama was able to use these principles of conformity and peer pressure[201] in his messages to get a larger audience to "try" him.

Marketing Implications of this chapter:

- Thoroughly understanding your customer is crucial before you begin selling to them. You can understanding your audience by asking them the following types of questions:

- What keeps them up at night?
- What do they desire above all else?
- What are they afraid of or angry about?
- What trends are occurring that will affect your audience?
- What are their top frustrations?

- You need to put all of your messages into the language of your audience. If they can't understand and identify with your brand, they probably won't buy from you either. People tend to buy from people just like them!

- When advertising or promoting your brand, remember that you must first woo your audience. Don't ask for the sale too quickly because they will likely spurn you. If instead you talk in terms of their interests and then offer your brand as a solution, you will have better success.

- Emotions lead to action. If your promotions can provide your audience with a strong emotional sentiment and trust for your brand, you are likely to create a feeling of liking and loyalty for your brand.[202] If the marketer can successfully tap into the emotions of the audience, then your audience is predisposed to believe whatever their emotions want them to believe.

- When using emotional advertising, you need to understand your audience's wishes and desires as well as their value systems. These lead to the consumer's appraisal of your brand as well as beliefs about your brand. The emotional responses from the appraisal lead to thoughts, arousal, expressions, and most importantly action.

- There are many values that most people share that you can use in your promotional efforts. These include:

- a preference for a less-pressured life

- a preference for an environment that is less threatening to their health

- a preference for a more meaningful, simpler life

- a preference for more solidarity and sharing experiences with others

- a preference for the preservation of the past rather than overthrowing things in the name of progress

- a preference for staying youthful looking rather than looking old.[203]

How can you use these common themes in your promotions?

- Emotions arise when there is an opportunity to enhance something your audience holds dear or threatens something that they hold dear. Barack Obama successfully agitated his audience's concerns as well as offered them hope for a better solution. What problems does your brand solve?

- You need to tie whatever you offer to your audience's value system. This is especially effective when you take advantage of the polarities in our lives.

- Reframing the situation can be a very effective strategy to redefine events in terms of your audience's values.

- If you want to do something new, it is more effective to stimulate your audience's imagination about experiencing something unique.

- Emotional pleasure comes from fantasizing about and anticipating experiencing the unique. Effective marketers feed the fantasy and curiosity about the unique experience.

- Consumers often identify with the pleasure of uplifting values. Don't just scare your audience; showing them how their lives can have more meaning and they can be part of something bigger is often a very effective promotion strategy. Showing your competence in creating and keeping positive feelings can lead to your audience preferring your brand.

- It is important to be congruent in all aspects of your marketing and provide your audience with positive appraisals of your brand at every opportunity. Remember to constantly reinforce your message. Repeated exposure to your brand enhances your audience's positive attitude toward your brand.

- Always provide testimonials or other examples of success in your promotion. Remember that most people like to follow the herd and need social proof before they make a decision. If you can get opinion leaders to support your brand, so much the better!

CHAPTER 15

Congruence of Tactics

If you've read this far, then you already know more about strategic branding than most of your competitors. We have discussed the importance of belief, understanding your audience, finding your role for the audience and the power of appealing to your audience's emotions through symbolism and emotional communication.

However, all of these techniques discussed will not help you much if you don't keep all of your marketing efforts congruent. Congruence is the idea that all parts of your marketing plan need to be a piece of a larger, single, whole. Think of congruence as building your symphony. While you may have wonderful strings, horns, and percussion sections, if they don't all fit with each other the overall sound will be a confusing (and headache-inducing) mess.

When your marketing efforts appear to be out of synch and do not reinforce each other your audience won't really know what your message is.

So it is with your branding efforts. Many politicians and businesses may have viable marketing tactics to deploy, but unless these tactics are congruent with each other you most likely will only confuse your audience. Many a marketer fails because he or she doesn't consistently deliver on the same theme. When your marketing efforts appear to be out of synch and do not reinforce each other your audience won't really know what your message is.

In order to be powerful, all of your tactics must reinforce the same theme. When you've decided upon your role and your story you want to convey, you need to ensure that you don't deviate from your message. When your audience is confused, they will not buy. The fifth step in the *Barack Marketing System* is **Congruence of Tactics**.

Barack Obama mastered the art of congruence throughout his presidential campaign. He accomplished this by understanding and using the classic marketing principles that makes your brand message cohesive. It is this congruence of tactics that will give your marketing punch the power that you need. Focus is key to success, especially when you are starting from a relatively obscure position. This section will discuss how Obama consistently delivered on his message and how you can use these same principles in your branding efforts.

CHAPTER 16

One Brand One Voice

*"Alongside our famous individualism, there's another ingre-
dient in the American saga. A belief that we are connected
as one people. If there's a child on the south side of
Chicago who can't read, that matters to me, even if it's not
my child. If there's a senior citizen somewhere who can't
pay for her prescription and has to choose between medi-
cine and the rent, that makes my life poorer, even if it's not
my grandmother. If there's an Arab American family being
rounded up without benefit of an attorney or due process,
that threatens my civil liberties. It's that fundamental
belief—I am my brother's keeper, I am my sister's
keeper—that makes this country work. It's what allows us to
pursue our individual dreams, yet still come together as a
single American family. E pluribus unum. Out of many, one."*

Barack Obama, Keynote Address at the
2004 Democratic National Convention, July 27, 2004[204]

The best branding campaign in the world won't amount
to much if it confuses your audience.[205] Too much or conflicting information is stifling for your audience. When people have too many choices, or the messages they hear conflict
with each other, then they will usually stop listening.

Therefore, it is central for the successful marketer to not
only deliver an appropriately themed story to his or her audience, but to make sure that the story is congruent in all of its
elements. All of your branding tactics have to work together
or your audience will most likely throw up their hands in sur-
render and move on to another brand that doesn't confuse
them (i.e., your competitor).

The 5 Cs of branding

The Barack Obama campaign understood the 5 Cs of
branding crucial to the *BARACK Marketing System*. If you

wish for your brand to stand out from the crowd, you need to understand and follow these five components of brand delivery as well. Namely, all of your brand messages must conform to the following rules:

1. All brand elements must be Clear.
2. All brand elements must be Connected.
3. All brand elements must be Complementary.
4. All brand elements must present a Comprehensive view of your brand.
5. All brand elements must be Consistently delivered and reinforced.

The most important aspect of your branding is that you clearly communicate your core story. When your audience doesn't understand your point, then it really doesn't matter what you do after that. We all need clarity in our lives. While we might be entertained by artistic branding without a message, we won't typically buy that brand.[206]

Clarity in your messages

A clear message is a simple one. While having a unique name for yourself or your product might help capture attention, you have to also make sure that your fundamental branding message is straightforward and easily understood. So, while Barack Obama's name actually could help serve to his advantage by suggesting that he was not an ordinary politician[207]; he actually distilled his campaign strategy into a few very short and memorable slogans that didn't require too much mental processing from his audience. The beauty of choosing slogans such as "Yes we can" was that they were easily remembered and allowed the audience to interpret them with their own meaning.[208] Of course, as we have already discussed, your message needs to be more than just a slogan if it is going to be truly successful. It must also show a unique promise of value to your audience.[209] By the time Barack

Obama was leading his audience in chants of "Yes we can" he had already established his identity in the mind of his audience as the leader of change.

So, while your branding messages must be clear, they must also be representative of your position in the market. The best branding messages come after you have already established your credibility with your audience. If you promote them too soon, you are likely to come off as just another person shouting a slogan without an original idea.

> **By the time Barack Obama was leading his audience in chants of "Yes We Can" he had already established his identity in the mind of his audience as the leader of change.**

Connected messages

Now that you have established simple clarity in your message (your unique selling proposition) you need to be certain that all of your messages are connected. Very often businesses and individuals will have various branding messages that don't seem to have much to do with each other. An organization might have one message and style for its print ads while using different messages and styles for websites, radio, etc. Connected branding tactics are crucial if you wish to present a cohesive message to your audience. For example, how many times have you called a company that 'cares about its customers' only to be put on terminal hold by a customer service representative? *In marketing, just like in dieting, EVERYTHING COUNTS.* When your branding messages are not connected across the various ways of delivery, then you have a mishmash of confusing signals. Which particular message should your audience listen to? Frankly, they're not going to spend the time to figure it out.

If you wish to put yourself at the front of the pack, you need to be sure that all of your branding messages are predictable and reliable. This means you must be sure all of your elements are connected without any branding surprises for your audience. Barack Obama and his campaign mastered the art of sending connected messages. While he did have some unique slogans (e.g., "Yes we can", "Hope", "Change you can believe in") they were all connected to his core message of him being the only one who could step in and change politics as usual.

The Obama team took this simple philosophy and propagated it throughout all of his marketing media including digital marketing, social media, viral marketing, database marketing, direct marketing, event marketing, targeted television, print and online advertising.[210] By connecting all of these elements with the same message, it didn't matter which forum his audience might come across. Obama's target market would get the same type of message regardless.

Complementary messages

Once you have established simple clear messages that are connected with each other, you need to ensure that all of your branding messages are complementary. Not every marketing message has to tell your entire story. Effective branders understand that each time you connect with your audience you might only be delivering a single piece of your message. In fact, for reasons stated earlier, you probably don't want to try to tell your entire story in one sitting. Smart marketers position their stories much the same way a television series would, one bite at a time. Yet, all the bites must be from the same meal.

In storytelling this would be known as a story arc.[211] Think of a scene in a movie. One individual scene might be a self-contained story, but it also serves to advance a larger story. Every time you deliver a marketing message, it not only needs to be self-contained but has to deliver on your larger story as well.

Barack Obama would use his speaking opportunities as vignettes in his larger story. Every time he spoke to an audience, he would tell his core message presented in a slightly different veneer. While it is nearly impossible to say everything you want to say in one sitting, small pieces presented over time do add up. While your branding messages should focus on only individual small, clear points, they do accumulate.

> *Every time you deliver a marketing message, it not only needs to be self-contained but has to deliver on your larger story as well. Barack Obama mastered complementary messaging in all aspects of his personal brand. In addition to his commercials, his manner of talk, as well as his words, helped to reinforce his core story of being the 'adult' in the room.*

Barack Obama was able to win over his audience in part because his branding efforts complemented each other. His manner of talk, as well as his words, helped to reinforce his core story of being the 'adult' in the room.[212] Obama even mastered his body language to reinforce these points as well.[213] Early in the Democratic primaries, many party supporters did not see Hillary Clinton's voice and mannerisms as being 'presidential.'[214] Given this, Barack Obama was able to convince supporters that he was a more viable candidate due in large part to the complementary nature of his persona, his writing, his speaking, and his message. Your audience will look for ALL parts of your image to complement the others as well. Your audience will paint a picture of you based on all of your different messages. While they don't have to be the same message over and over, all pieces of your branding puzzle must fit together into a whole.

Comprehensive messages

In a similar vein to your marketing messages being complementary, they must also be comprehensive. Because successful marketers take their core story and break it into bite-sized chunks, you must be sure that all of the bites are delivered. If you are missing elements of your brand story you

will not come across as a complete brand. In order to successfully pull this off, you need to determine two things:

1.   What are all of the necessary messages you need to
     convey in order to present a full and complete pic-
     ture of your brand?, and
2.   What are the various media your audience will use
     to access your brand messages?

It is very important that your audience gets a full and
complete picture of who you are and your value proposition.
If large segments of your audience are missing pieces of the
puzzle, then they obviously will not see and understand your
entire story. So, while you want to present small complementary pieces of your brand buffet to your audience, be sure that
everyone leaves with a complete meal!

Barack Obama understood his core audience and what
they wanted to hear. Throughout his interaction with them he
was able to present pieces of the Obama puzzle that led up to
a complete picture of the candidate (at least as much of a complete picture as his audience wanted). One of the most effective strategies Obama used to accomplish this was through his
book tour for <u>The Audacity of Hope</u>. Obama mixed campaign stops with this book tour allowing him to refine his
message and test the waters while getting his manifesto out to
the public.[215] During this book signing tour, Obama successfully presented various pieces of his manifesto tailored to local
situations. However, when looked at overall, a more complete picture of his story began to emerge. Through reading
his book and reports of his various campaign stops, his audience would acquire a more complete picture of his brand even
though they might have only seen one small facet themselves.

> *While you want to present small complementary pieces
> of your brand buffet to your audience, be sure that
> everyone leaves with a complete meal! During his book
> signing tour, Obama successfully presented various
> pieces of his manifesto tailored to local situations.*

However, when looked at overall, a more complete picture of his story began to emerge.

In addition, the Barack Obama campaign managed to present a comprehensive branding strategy through the very effective use of many (and different) advertising and marketing venues. The Obama campaign was one of the first to make very effective use of Web 2.0 technology.[216] Using a combination of traditional and viral marketing allowed the campaign to be sure to target all likely voters in a manner that was most comfortable to them. Barack Obama targeted younger voters early in the campaign primarily through effective use of the internet.[217] As his campaign (and his audience) matured, he had amassed enough money to buy as much traditional advertising as he could desire, culminating in his 30-minute infomercial aired during the end of the general election.[218]

While Obama's core message did not change from his earlier campaign days, the venues he used would. By snowballing his early success, Obama was able to deliver his messages through pretty much any outlet conceivable, including in-game advertising.[219] If you can present your branding messages in the manner your audience likes to receive them, then you will be on your way. As your brand and your business grow you can begin expanding the venues used for your message delivery.

Consistency in your messages and delivery

Last, the most effective branding strategy won't work unless you are consistent across your messages and delivery. While individual messages don't have to be the same to be effective, they do need to all be from the same tree as it were. So, complementary messages are fine because they are all parts of the same whole. Inconsistent messages on the other hand will lead your audience to distrust you and shop your competition.

Whenever you tell your brand story, you must deliver a consistent theme. As discussed earlier, people will ultimately judge you by the truth of your message. Your message is the core of your brand story and this message cannot change without running the risk of losing your audience. It is indeed perfectly acceptable for you to change individual messages, but you can't change the core message they are delivering. Successful advertisers and marketers don't change themes, just presentation of themes. So while you might have different commercials with different appeals, at the end of the day they had better tell the same story.

Barack Obama understood the power of consistency throughout his campaign. Very early on he created a logo that was easily identifiable. Obama's famous rising sun logo was designed to portray his message visually.[220] Like any good marketer, he stamped this logo (or slight variations of it) everywhere he went. Whenever Barack Obama spoke you would see his logo systematically displayed.[221]

> **Whenever you tell your brand story, you must deliver a consistent theme. People will ultimately judge you by the truth of your message. Your message is the core of your brand story and this message cannot change without running the risk of losing your audience. It is indeed perfectly acceptable for you to change individual messages, but you can't change the core message they are delivering.**

One of the unique aspects of an Obama campaign rally was the consistency throughout the signage used in the audience. Whereas many politicians are content to have their name or slogan slapped on any poster-board or bumper sticker, Obama's message was consistently showcased in the crowd. You did not see as many homemade signs at his rally because this would confuse his message. Tight control over the colors, fonts, logos and slogans ensured his consistency in his branding material.[222]

You could see a great deal of cohesion across all of his marketing media down to the level of the fonts his campaign used.[223] In fact, graphic designers went so far as to point out that his choice of the Gotham font for all of his marketing collateral (signs, print, websites, etc.) became synonymous with his brand.[224] The Gotham font had been designed to appear masculine and fresh and Barack Obama used this to his advantage.

The Obama campaign also primarily used blue throughout its marketing media, perhaps with a subtle nod to making the electoral map bluer in November. Even the images of Obama that were used in his branding messages followed the same theme. Obama would consistently be shown as looking upward with a heavenly glow. *In his campaign material Obama was seldom seen looking directly at the camera so as not to appear too threatening. Instead, the images helped to serve the cool and larger-than-life persona that Barack Obama was cultivating through his core story.*[225]

The Barack Obama campaign did not stop with his logo and campaign signage. Web designs were consistently applied and replicated. Tools were provided to his core audience to help spread his message consistently. While Obama did allow his famous O logo to be slightly modified to suit the needs of any particular audience, they were all variations on a theme.[226] So, while you could detect slight changes of the logo being used from students to sportsmen, the overarching symbol was the same (i.e., the rising sun over the farmland of America). By allowing this sort of directed message while staying on theme, *Obama allowed his supporters to support him in their own way while retaining tight control over his message at the same time.*

Even after winning the presidential election Barack Obama continued to brand himself in a consistent manner. In order to help expand his message even further, the Democratic National Committee created Organizing for America designed for citizens to help support the President's agenda.[227] When looking at this website you will see the same colors, fonts and motifs he used so successfully throughout the election process.

Of course, the consistency in Barack Obama's brand did not stop with the physical fonts, logos, signs and websites. The man himself was known to be incredibly consistent with how he portrayed himself throughout the campaign. Coming across as "unruffable", Obama managed to project his aura of cool (some would say aloof) assuredness.[228] Some bloggers even went so far as to point out the consistency of the Obama smile![229] The image Barack Obama projected was nothing if not consistent. If you wish for your brand to be successful, you must be consistent as well.

> **The image Barack Obama projected was nothing if not consistent. If you wish for your brand to be successful, you must be consistent as well.**

Marketing Implications of this chapter:

- All of your hard work understanding your audience and satisfying their yearnings with your story will be for nothing if you don't follow the 5 C's of branding!

- A confused consumer does not buy.

- When creating your marketing messages always stay true to your core story. However, remember the following points:

    - Each individual marketing message should be clear and understandable to your audience.

    - It's okay to have multiple bite-sized marketing messages. Just be sure that they are all telling parts of the same story.

    - Be sure to include ALL parts of your brand story with your individual messages. The messages should complement each other.

    - DO NOT have multiple messages that tell different stories. Each message has to somehow be connected to the other messages. They are all parts of the same whole.

- All of your marketing messages should tell the COMPLETE story. It's okay to have different messages tell different pieces, but you need to make sure to not leave out any pieces of your story or you will lose your audience.

  - Your marketing messages need to be consistent across time and place. Namely, they must tell the same story. The more control you exert over how you are seen by your audience, the better for your story.

- Not only do all of your message elements have to be consistent with each other, they need to be consistent with your core story. If your core story is that you are friendly and approachable but your logo appears as formal you are sending mixed signals that will confuse your audience.

- Your branding story is never really over. Even after you've "won" your audience you need to stay on task with all of your messages and communication with them.

- Remember, when it comes to branding, EVERY-THING COUNTS. Be sure to focus on ALL aspects of your business or brand. This includes (but is not limited to):

  - Your written marketing collateral

  - Your audio and visual material

  - Your physical place of business

  - Your website

  - Your employees

  - YOU!

CHAPTER 17

Step 6: Kindle Your Community

If you've taken the time to read this far, and follow the guidelines set forth, then you are well on your way to building a successful brand – in time. In today's world though, it is important to understand that brands **CAN** be built almost overnight. If you don't learn how to build your brand at internet speed it is entirely possible that you will have a long and illustrious career. However, it is also entirely possible that you will be left in the dust by others who understand the power of community and building a brand rapidly.

In politics, the conventional wisdom for seeking a presidential nomination had always been to pay your dues. By working within the system, making connections and gaining a reputation you could parlay you could seek the support of your party. When Barack Obama entered the presidential race he encountered very well-known politicians who were also seeking the presidency. The others (especially Hillary Clinton) had vast political machines and resources behind them. They were the entrenched competition. Yet Obama prevailed. How?

By following the same principles that you can learn to progress your career or business. Barack Obama learned and mastered the power of building a community quickly. By following both classic and modern marketing techniques, he was able to harness the power of the internet combined with ages-old human nature. This potent combination was enough to fire up his audience and have them spread his message faster and more effectively than he could have ever hoped to on his own.

If you don't learn how to build your brand at internet speed it is entirely possible that you will have a long and illustrious career. However, it is also entirely possible

that you will be left in the dust by others who under-stand the power of community and building a brand rapidly.

The last step in the **BARACK *Marketing System*** is to learn how to **Kindle Your Community.** You need to ignite the passion in your audience and give them the tools to spread your message like wildfire. Today, people want and expect instantaneous results. You need to learn how to capitalize on your audience's enthusiasm and excitement and take them to immediate action.

It is this last step that gives your brand the momentum to rise to the top of a market in short order. The tools and techniques are readily available for anybody who would like to use them. Learn them. Use them. And you too will be able to dominate your market through the power of building loyal and raving fans almost overnight.

CHAPTER 18

Marketing in an Internet World

*"And if you will join me in this improbable quest, if you feel
destiny calling, and see as I see, a future of endless possi-
bility stretching before us; if you sense, as I sense, that the
time is now to shake off our slumber, and slough off our
fear, and make good on the debt we owe past and future
generations, then I'm ready to take up the cause, and
march with you, and work with you. Together, starting
today, let us finish the work that needs to be done, and
usher in a new birth of freedom on this Earth."*

Barack Obama, – announcing his candidacy for the presidency

Winning is always easier with allies. While many successful people like to believe that they are entirely self-made,
this is usually far from the truth. In today's world it is rare, if
not impossible, to make it on your own. This is especially true
in the fields of politics and business. By definition, a politician
cannot be elected to office without the support of the voters.
By definition, a business person cannot make any money
without the support of customers.

So, while it might be nice to pretend that we are solely
independent, we are not. The sooner we recognize this simple
reality the sooner we can learn to identify the stakeholders in
our success and harness them to help advance our cause. This
is exactly what Barack Obama did to get elected President of
the United States. It is what you need to do as well if you wish
to rise to the top of your industry or profession.

In today's world it is rare, if not impossible, to make it
on your own. The key to modern business success then is to
build a community of your own. You need your own loyal
audience who is invested in your success every bit as much
as you are invested in theirs.

The importance of building a community

In today's era, if you want true success in business you must build a community and build it rapidly. What is a community in business? Basically the same thing as the community you live in. In business a community is a group of people who share a common goal and aspirations. Members of the community are somehow connected to each other and have a stake in the success of each other. When a member of the community falters, it can drag down others in the community, so the community has self-interest to ensure its survival and growth. The key to modern business success then is to build a community of your own. You need your own loyal audience who is invested in your success every bit as much as you are invested in theirs.

The question arises then, how should the modern marketer best build and harness the power of a community? Think of building a community the same way you built friendships growing up. The most common way of building a community is one person at a time. You want to show your audience how their interests are best served by allying themselves with you. *This can be accomplished by following the principles set forth in this book (i.e., understand your audience's needs, find what they yearn for, and position your story to show them how you are the only logical choice to deliver what they want).*

Building a community rapidly

The problem with building a community in this fashion is that it can take a great deal of time and effort to create a large community if we approach our audience one at a time. While it is entirely possible (and even likely) that you will build strong relationships with your audience this way, it is doubtful that you will grow your brand on a large scale. Building relationships one at a time is powerful but not very efficient. You need to harness the power of relationships and community but also do so on a larger scale and in a rapid manner.

So, how do we do this? Well, let's go back to high school. Let's say that you're sixteen and your family just moved to a new town. You want to make some friends quickly. You can single out the one, two, or three other kids who look like they might be compatible with you and work on developing relationships with them. If successful you will probably end up with two or three very good friends. This is wonderful, but it's not going to skyrocket your brand name. So, you decide on a different strategy. You pick out the one or two "cool" kids in the school and befriend them. Once you've done this, well now you have the power of tapping into their pre-existing social groups and you suddenly find your stock in school rising rapidly.

The community followers will often defer to the opinion leaders. So, if you can get some opinion leaders to support your brand the followers will join the bandwagon.

The world of politics and business is not really all that different from high school. One of the best ways to build a community rapidly is to find the "cool" kids (or as we would say in business, the opinion leaders) and befriend them. The reality is that most people are followers. If you can gain the support of the community leaders, then a great portion of the community will follow right after them. The community followers make decisions based on how other trusted people (opinion leaders) have made decisions in the past.[230] The community followers will often defer to the opinion leaders. So, if you can get some opinion leaders to support your brand the followers will join the bandwagon.

This is exactly what Barack Obama did when he began his quest for the Democratic Party nomination. Like any good politician, Obama sought out key endorsements early in his presidential quest. Two key endorsements from Missouri Senator Claire McCaskill and Massachusetts Senator Teddy

Kennedy came very early in his campaign.[231] These endorsements helped position Obama as being acceptable to Democratic women (who had primarily been lining up behind Hillary Clinton) and the liberal wing of the Democratic Party.

Know who your opinion leaders are

Yet the Obama campaign had done something different as well. While all politicians seek endorsements from other politicians, Barack Obama sought endorsements from opinion leaders throughout the various audiences he was courting. The Obama campaign made an early and crucial decision to take his campaign straight to the people through the use of the internet.[232] This allowed existing internet communities to spread his message. Through the use of blogs and other social media tools, Obama was able to capture endorsements from online opinion leaders helping spread his early message far and wide.[233] In fact, one of the key endorsements Barack Obama received very early on in his campaign was that of Chris Hughes, one of the founders of Facebook.[234] Mr. Hughes was instrumental in helping the Obama campaign manage their social media message that would be such a factor in his success.

And of course, Barack Obama also gained another key asset; he was able to win the hearts of many members of the mass media. Pundits and reporters were among the early proponents of Barack Obama. Even in his early political career, Barack Obama was able to garner the support of reporters and other people of influence. Very early on he developed fans in the media who helped fan the flames for him in his run for office.[235]

People with a forum are well-positioned to help spread your message to the larger audience, and this is exactly what these people did. Throughout his campaign many wondered how Obama was so successful at winning the support of influential people, especially among commentators and the news industry.[236] When looked at somewhat more closely though, this does make a certain amount of sense. It is a common mis-conception among marketers to treat business-to-business marketing as different from business to consumer marketing. Essentially, while reporters and pundits do indeed work for various organizations, and one would therefore assume that the needs of the organization are what motivate them, we can-not lose sight of the fact that organizations are comprised of people. The same things that motivate people as individuals also motivate them within their organizational setting. There-fore it should not be surprising to realize that newscasters are actually people each with their own unique perspectives and proclivity to understand and buy into the stories that are being told to them. When looked at in this light, it is easier to understand how these newscasters and commentators would support a story which they personally believe in as well.[237]

> *The same things that motivate people as individuals also motivate them within their organizational setting. If you are seeking to have opinion leaders in the media sup-port you, it would help if your core story matches their personal beliefs.*

Get your audience leaders to identify themselves and take action on your behalf

While gaining the support of key opinion-leaders is a surefire way to help launch your brand, Barack Obama's cam-paign recognized that there was more to it. Basically, we know that support of opinion leaders will help grow our brand and reputation, but how do we garner this support; or, if it were so easy why isn't everyone doing it?

The key is to identify opinion leaders who are the most receptive to your message. And, the people most likely to be receptive to your message early on will usually organize around their interests and voluntarily calling themselves out of the crowd.[238] The Obama campaign recognized this and sought out on-line interest groups who would be the most likely to receive the Obama brand message (such as students and young voters).[239] In addition, Obama's campaign made early and effective use of organizers. These people often idealized Obama's own early community organizer days and were encouraged to tell their personal stories to voters. Many of these people were moved either by Obama himself, or a greater concern for the country or the planet. Discussing hopes, fears, and dreams the Obama community at times *"sounded like a giant self-help group where the therapy was politics."*[240]

Having early supporters share their personal stories bought another advantage for Barack Obama. The more you can get your customers to elaborate upon the experience they have with you or your product, the more likely you are to make it a memorable experience for them. People are more committed to those things that they take a public stand on.[241] Also, telling their stories created a strong sense of involvement for Obama's early supporters. The more involved somebody is with your brand, the more likely they are to help promote it to others.[242] A second benefit to publicly telling your story is that once people have taken a public stand on an issue, it is increasingly difficult to get them to change their minds. The Obama campaign was very effective at getting people to commit early to the candidate and to publicly endorse him to others.[243] By doing this Obama helped ensure that these people would remain loyal to him.

By allowing his supporters the opportunity to act and ACT NOW Barack Obama was able to get on-line community leaders to become organizers and promoters of his brand. The Obama team then very smartly provided the tools his audience needed to take immediate action in showing their support for him.

Last, Barack Obama and his team mastered the art of quick action when it came to asking his audience for commitment. As discussed, Obama had learned the art of emotional marketing and used this to great success. Emotions are essentially impulses to act. **When you can engage someone emotionally in your message, NOW is the time to get them to do**

something about it. Emotions are best tied into experiences.[244]   By allowing his supporters the opportunity to act and ACT NOW Barack Obama was able to get on-line community leaders to become organizers and promoters of his brand.   The Obama team then very smartly provided the tools his audience needed to take immediate action in showing their support for him.[245]

Once early supporters started organizing and promoting on Obama's behalf, Obama's message quickly spread through his core audience. Greg Stielstra likens creating and spreading a brand message to starting a fire.[246] First you need to focus on the driest kindling (i.e., the most receptive and passionate audience), second you need to start the fire by giving these people an experience with the product, third you need to spread the fire which allows the people who are the new believers of your brand to spread the message for you, and last you need to keep a record of who you've done business with so that you can contact them again (saving the coals). The use of internet technology and social media only served to spread the Obama brand faster and further than it otherwise would have.

Online communities are different than other communities (and the same)

Much has been made of how Barack Obama used the internet for good reason – it worked! Barack Obama's campaign was successful primarily not because it got a lot of people out to vote, but it got people to get *others* out to vote.[247] Barack Obama had learned how to position his core story to his audience such that his story could be interpreted by them into their own personal stories. His campaign was not so much about policy but about 'hope' and 'change' which were terms that allowed his audience to understand in their own ways. Therefore, his story encouraged his audience to make and share it as their own story. The Obama campaign gave unrestricted permission for its audience to share, post, and repurpose any and all campaign material that was posted on its website, thus enabling volunteers to create their own Obama messages and communities.

> **Barack Obama's early campaign was not so much about policy but about 'hope' and 'change' which were terms that allowed his audience to understand in their own ways. Therefore, his story encouraged his audience to make and share it as their own story.**

That Barack Obama's brand spread rapidly should therefore come as no surprise. When Obama had announced his candidacy, it was estimated that there were over 220 million internet users in the United States. A great majority of these users are connected to other users and were used to sharing great quantities of information with very little effort.[248] By providing them with the branding tools they needed (that of course had been created as discussed previously) Barack Obama allowed his audience to spread his message literally at the touch of a button.

Like any Web 2.0 savvy marketer, Obama's team took full advantage of the psychology and technology of today's world. There has been a seismic shift in how people like to receive marketing information as well as the implications of this.[249] Improvements in internet technology have transferred the power from the organization to the consumer on the web. This was a key piece to the success of Barack Obama. In practical terms, this means:

- Internet technology has created new home-grown authority figures such as bloggers and on-line pundits, rather than ones put forth by organizations.

- There has been a migration of opinion and thought leadership to consumers and a great deal of propagation in the numbers of these leaders.

- Internet technology has allowed mash-ups of technologies and message. Evidence of this could be seen in the 'Obama Girl' videos as well as many graphics and ads where Obama's audience used his message to create and spread their own versions.

- Internet technology allows for the ability for your message to go viral. This is both good and bad because now your message can spread rapidly, but you can also lose control of it as well.

Principles don't change – context does

Successful marketers understand that while marketing principles don't change, the context in which they are applied does. The shift of power from the organization to the consumer is one that Barack Obama well understood. Other aspects of this shift are that your audience can and will distribute your message in unique ways that they determine; not necessarily in ways that you had originally intended. Furthermore, new technology leads to richer online experiences and content for the user, as well as the breaking down of barriers between PCs, phones, and mobile devices. *Bottom line: your audience can and will experience their web content in many different ways.* Just as Barack Obama did, you would be best served by understanding this and providing your audience the tools they need to experience your brand the way you intend.

> **Successful marketers understand that while marketing principles don't change, the context in which they are applied does.**

Basically, the rise of Web2.0 allows for consumers to request their marketing messages rather than having these messages forced on them. This was a critical factor in the early stages of the Obama campaign.[250] Barack Obama allowed his audience to share his message amongst themselves in their own way helping to give it the necessary fidelity (the 'stamp of approval') they required for its authenticity. This

was accomplished through alerts, feeds, blogs and other internet marketing techniques.[251]   Only after Obama had built his
loyal fan base did he put forth his message through massive
TV and other advertising.

Knowing your numbers helps dramatically

The Barack Obama team also recognized that the most
effective use of internet technology wasn't just for existing
communities to spread their messages. While this alone can
help send your brand to the top of your market, you would be
leaving the true power of technology behind. For it wasn't
just the viral messaging that helped grow Barack Obama's
brand. Correct use of internet technology allows the successful marketer to control and grow his or her brand with preci-
sion and speed. Barack Obama's team knew and used this
power.

One of the most misunderstood (and therefore misused)
aspects of internet technology is the use of metrics and targeting.
If you merely take your brand and unleash in on the internet
community, they might indeed spread your message for you. If
you're lucky, it will even be the message you want spread! The
problem with this type of viral marketing is that you can easily
lose control of your message, which is a serious no-no to the
BARACK Marketing System student.   When your audience
totally takes over your story, well, all bets are off.

Therefore, if you want to be truly successful with growing your brand at internet speed, you must make sure that you
spread your story (especially at the beginning) to the right
people. You need to identify those who are most receptive to
your message and use these people (the insiders) to spread
your message to their followers. This will help keep your message authentic to both yourself and your audience.

> **If you merely take your brand and unleash in on the
> internet community, they might indeed spread your mes-
> sage for you. If you're lucky, it will even be the message
> you want spread!**

Essentially, you need to be sure that you are correctly targeting and following up with your core audience if you wish for them to spread your message in the manner you desire. The Barack Obama team recognized this and therefore made extensive use of target marketing and marketing metrics (the measurements that tell you whether or not your marketing efforts are succeeding). Listen to the words of Obama's campaign manager, David Plouffe:

"One of the beauties of technology and data is that you can track the contribution history and volunteer performance of people all the way through the campaign. On November 4, 2008, we knew how much each person at the Austin rally had performed through the entire campaign. How many times did they contribute? Did they volunteer? Did they vote in the Texas primary and attend the Texas caucus? Are they part of an online group? This type of data made establishing metrics much easier and allows us to track what people responded to and what they didn't.[252]"

The power of rituals and incentives

The Barack Obama campaign team also learned to use rituals in their branding campaigns. It is well known that rituals have power.[253] Various marketing messages constantly encouraged Obama's supporters to leave their computer terminals and interact with fellow supporters through "Countdown to Change" parties and other venues.[254] The group interaction of these events would only serve to reinforce the support of Obama's core audience. In addition, these opportunities were a way to help rally the troops around specific issues and causes that the Obama campaign had targeted (in an almost immediate fashion).

Constant communication with his audience (via e-mail, Twitter, and Facebook, among others) allowed Barack Obama to provide his audience with the tools they needed to spread his message. It also allowed the campaign to ask for small favors such as small campaign contributions, or forwarding email messages to their friends. These messages could be targeted to the specific groups that the Obama team was courting. Asking for small targeted favors, combined with the ability for Barack Obama's core supporters to ask their friends and connections for similar favors helped create the 'grassroots' movement so critical to Obama's rapid success.

Especially when combined with incentives, asking for small favors can entice your audience to action. For example the Indiana 3-on-3 challenge offered any student in Indiana who helped register 20 of his friends to vote to be entered in a drawing to play a game of 3-on-3 basketball against Barack Obama.[255] Highlights of this game were then videotaped and uploaded to various blogs and social networking sites. The campaign itself resulted in 150,000 newly registered voters in Indiana as well as providing more messaging for Obama's supporters to enjoy and share. So, as can be seen, when done successfully small favors can lead to big results.

The power of kindling your community is crucial if you wish to grow your brand far and wide. Early on and throughout his campaign, Barack Obama made extensive use of internet technology, including but not limited to Facebook, Twitter, MySpace, YouTube, and his own websites. Because these existing forums had built-in communities, Obama was able to tap into their power and grow his fan base at unprecedented speeds (at least for politicians). While Barack Obama had already established his voice and story, internet technology and culture made it possible for him to create a volunteer sales force to grow his brand with unprecedented speed.

Marketing Implications of this chapter:

- While you very well might build a powerful brand without community support (especially if you follow the principles laid out in the BARACK marketing system), your brand is likely to languish unless you enlist allies to your cause.

- The best allies are the opinion-leaders in their respective fields. The more you can get people who already have other people's ear to advocate for you, the faster you will grow your social network.

- Along these lines, the first supporters you seek will ideally have their own forum from which they speak. Identify the key group(s) you would like to target with your message and seek out the existing forums that already serve the group(s). Chances are that one or two individuals will rise to the top as the community elders of the group. These are the people that the group listens to and who you would be well-advised to have endorse you.

- Remember that even opinion-leaders who work for organizations are still people. Approach them as you would individually, namely, in terms of their own personal interests. Try as they might, most people cannot separate their personal feelings from 'corporate objectiveness.' Understand, and use, this principle.

- When looking for allies to spread your brand message, be sure that they can modify your core story to suit their individual stories. As discussed in previous chapters, your most loyal (and therefore vocal) supporters will be those who see your message as part of their core story. Marketing principles prevail; people think in terms of their own self-interest. Show your audience how supporting you provides them benefit.

- The more you can get members of your community to publicly commit to you, the better.

- In a similar fashion, the more you can get members of your community to take actions (even small ones) on your behalf, the better.

- Ritual events (online and offline) help solidify your community. What can you provide your community that is ritualistic?

- Remember the power of the internet, both for good and bad:

  - Consumer experiences with organizations have changed due to internet technology. More and more the true power is in the hands of the consumer, not the organization.

  - Consumers are more likely to take your message, modify it for their purposes, and share it with other members of the community because of these technologies and the internet culture.

  - If you don't allow your audience to shape and share your message, they can revolt against you.

  - If you allow your audience to control your message, they can destroy you.

  - Therefore, provide your audience with the tools they need to shape and share your message while still staying true to all of your branding efforts. Your branding must always stay true to your core story.

- Be sure to collect marketing metrics along the way. If you can't target and identify your community, then you won't be as successful in following up with them and providing them with what they want.

- Incentives work. Just be sure to gear them to the interests of your audience. Be creative; it's not always about money (in fact, it's usually not about money).

- The internet is big today. Will it still be big tomorrow? Probably, but who really knows for sure. Two things we do know:

  - Technology will always be changing, so you need to understand it if you wish to harness it, and;

- Even when technology changes people are people and communities are communities. Classic marketing principles are evergreen. Stay true to these principles, understand the environment you are working in, and go forth and brand!

CHAPTER 19

Delivering the Promise

> *"Making your mark on the world is hard. If it were easy, everybody would do it. But it's not. It takes patience, it takes commitment, and it comes with plenty of failure along the way. The real test is not whether you avoid this failure, because you won't. It's whether you let it harden or shame you into inaction, or whether you learn from it; whether you choose to persevere."*
>
> BARACK OBAMA, speech, Jul. 12, 2006

Audiences can be very fickle. One day they'll love you and the next day they'll hate you. You can't trust your customers to remain loyal to you because as soon as the next best thing comes along they'll leave you in a heartbeat, right? WRONG! People aren't as fickle as you'd like to imagine. Of course it is entirely possible that your customers will leave you. When they do, remember one simple reality; it's probably something you did.

The bottom line, your audience isn't necessarily fickle, but then again, they don't want to feel like they've been lied to. And that's exactly how they will feel if you don't deliver on the big promise that you make them. When your audience senses that you might be a fraud, they will turn on you like a pack of hungry dogs on a t-bone steak.

> *After you've acquired your supporters it is entirely possible that they will leave you. When they do, remember one simple reality; it's probably something you did.*

Therefore, it is crucial that you deliver on your promise and remain true to your core story that successfully sold you in the first place. The entire point to the **BARACK Marketing System** is to truly understand the deep, emotional needs of your audience and deliver to your audience a story that will help them resolve these needs. Central to this though is the idea that you also have to have absolute fidelity to your (and your audience's) story and follow through on the promises you make.

Today's consumers don't like to be sold to in the traditional sense. We are in an era of relationship marketing, where your audience wants to feel that you are truly a partner in their success. Your audience doesn't want to feel that you are using them for your own personal gain but that both they and you can benefit from working together. *Most people will not begrudge your brand being successful, as long as you also make them successful as well (and no, success doesn't have to mean money, although that is always nice).*

Basically what this all boils down to: once you've gotten people to think of you as the solution to their problem, YOU HAD BETTER DELIVER! Now, what about the occasional screw-up that you are likely to make along the way? The true power in delivering the promise is that (if you've been following the **BARACK Marketing System**) by now you have developed a deep and emotional bond with your audience. As long as the story and solution you've told are truth that you believe in you most likely have established a strong relationship with your audience.

> **Basically what this all boils down to is: Once you've gotten people to think of you as the solution to their problem, YOU HAD BETTER DELIVER!**

If you have a relationship with your audience, then they will forgive you the minor mistake, just as you would hope anybody in a committed relationship would. Too many minor mistakes (or a couple of big ones) though will cause your audience to question their relationship with you. *When you stay true to your audience you will retain their loyalty. Turn away from them and they will turn away from you.*

Marketing Implications of this chapter:

- The successful marketer knows that gaining a client, customer, or fan is only the first step. You are now at the beginning of your relationship.

- Like any solid relationship, mutual trust from both parties is paramount to its success:

    - You must always stay true to your core story.

    - You must keep the promises you make to your audience

- If you are unable to deliver on the promises you make, find an alternative way to help your audience find their fulfillment.

- Always keep in contact with your audience. Information exchange is at the heart of a good relationship.

- You will likely make some blunders along the way as your brand grows. That's okay. People will forgive honest mistakes, but not if they feel they've been lied to. So, don't lie in your promises.

- Earn the loyalty of your audience by always delivering, as best as possible, and staying true and you will have fans for life.

CHAPTER 20

The End of the Story?

> *"Our challenges may be new. The instruments with which we meet them may be new. But those values upon which our success depends — honesty and hard work, courage and fair play, tolerance and curiosity, loyalty and patriotism — these things are old. These things are true. They have been the quiet force of progress throughout our history. What is demanded, then, is a return to these truths."*
>
> BARACK OBAMA, Inaugural Address, Jan. 20. 2009

And so, with the scepter of the secret in hand, the handsome new king took the reins of power and began to rule the kingdom. Through war and peace. Through feast and famine. Through good times and bad. The King stayed loyal and true to his subjects guiding them with a loving, but firm, hand. Always listening to the will of the people, and always treasuring their secret, the King obtained amazing results for the kingdom. The new King ushered in an era of peace, prosperity, and happiness for both himself and the people the likes of which had never before been seen. Remaining constantly faithful to each other, the King and his people supported and loved each other and remained ever loyal. And they all lived happily ever after.

ALTERNATE ENDING:

And so, with the scepter of the secret in hand, the handsome new king took the reins of power and began to rule the kingdom. Through war and peace. Through feast and famine. Through good times and bad. And yet, along the way, the King stopped listening to the people. Having obtained the crown, he no longer stayed true to the secret for it no longer mattered to him. Walled off in his castle, the King lost sight of the secret of the people that had led to his power. The people shouted, but the king did not listen for he had forgotten how. More and more isolated each day, the King lost touch with his subjects and they, in turn, no longer trusted him to lead. Having obtained his position, the King believed he had all of the power. He would merely force his will upon the people. And yet, it was the people who had the power. They sought new princes and princesses who would wrest the kingdom from the newly despised king. With the support of the people the new princes and princesses removed the King. And they all lived happily ever after (except for the king).

The story of Barack Obama's Presidency is yet to be written. Yet the lessons from the story of his election are clear. By understanding the steps outlined in this book, you can see how Barack Obama was able to rise from relative obscurity to a household name. The secrets to this aren't really secret. They are classic marketing truths that have been known and used for some time by successful marketers.

How will your story be told?

How will your story be told? Will your brand be one that obtains and retains a loyal audience for years into the future? Or will you acquire and then lose your following? Perhaps you'll never gain a following at all.

Like all truly powerful stories, the story of the election of Barack Obama to the Presidency of the United States has a clearly defined beginning, middle, and end. The story of his Presidency is yet to be written. By understanding the steps outlined in this book, you can see how Barack Obama was able to rise from relative obscurity to a household name. The secrets to this aren't really secret. They are classic marketing truths that have been known and used for some time by successful marketers.

Truths are truths, regardless of where or how they are told. Barack Obama and his team were able to use these truths to obtain market dominance. You, too, can use these principles if you are looking to send yourself or your brand to the top of your market or discipline. While contexts and players change, the fundamental principles do not. This book has outlined many of the classic marketing principles used by Barack Obama to obtain his success. Understanding and using the BARACK Marketing System can allow you to obtain your own.

Marketing principles are timeless

Always **Believe** in yourself and your cause. If you don't, then frankly, you shouldn't be pursuing it. Always understand the yearnings of your **Audience**. Learn to think like they do. Learn to listen.

Identify your **Role** in relationship to your audience. Know who you are and what you stand for. Most importantly, know how your role fulfills the story that your audience is living. Know what solution you provide your audience, and always stay faithful to your role.

Once you've identified your role, understand the emotional **Aspirations** of your audience and deliver your solution accordingly. All people want fulfillment in their lives. In fact that's the only reason we 'purchase' anything; to fulfill a need or desire that we have. Show your audience how your brand can fulfill them in terms that they understand.

Never forget to be **Congruent** in all of your branding efforts. Follow the 5 Cs of branding as outlined in this book. DO NOT confuse your audience, for a confused mind does not buy.

Last, be sure to **Kindle your community**. Find and embrace your allies. Create loyal fans that will help spread your message far and wide ensuring your rapid and far-reaching success.

If you remain truthful to the steps outlined in the BARACK Marketing System, then success will *be* yours. If you remain truthful to yourself, your audience, and your story, then success will *stay* yours.

Resources:

Thank you for taking the time to read this book. If you would like to know more about the following topics, please see the recommended resources.

For information on storytelling and how to use it in your business, visit my website at: www.storytrek.com.

For information on archetypes and character development, visit my website at: www.rolemarketing.com

For more information on Barack Obama and the topics discussed in this book, please visit my website at: www.BrandItLikeBarack.com

If you would like information on the BARACK Marketing System and how you could use it in your business or professional life, please visit my website at: www.theBARACK marketingSystem.com

If you would like to contact me, please send an email to GKaskowitz@branditlikebarack.com.

References:

"Hit Or Miss: How Will 2008 Be Remembered in Marketing Circles?." marketingnews Monday/15 Dec. 2008: 18-19.

"Once Upon a Time: When a Meeting Ofthe Minds Isn't Enough,try a Meeting of Theemotions: Tell a Story.." Strategy & Business Wednesday/10 Apr. 2002: 1-5.

"The Rise and Fall of Brand Hillary." Adweek Monday/3 Mar. 2008: 34-35.

About Organizing for America. 2009. Democratic National Committee. Available: http://www.barackobama.com/learn/about_ofa.php 2010.

Barack Obama - Words That Inspired a Nation. . New York: Fall River Press, 2009.

Barack Obama Quotes. 2010. Available: http://www.notable-quotes.com/o/obama_barack.html. 2/4/2010 2010.

Dobbs Asked If Obama Is "Pandering to Ethnocentric Special Interests Again" By Accepting Richardson's Endorsement. 2008. Available: http://mediamatters.org/research/200803240009. 2/4/2010 2010.

Excerpts From an Interview With Barack Obama. 2007. The New York Times. Available: http://www.nytimes.com/2007/10/27/us/politics/28q-aobama.html. 8/13/2009 2009.

Fainting Rallies. 2008. Available: http://www.dailymotion.com/video/x4eaod_fainting-rallies_news. 2/4/2010 2010.

Illinois Sen. Barack Obama's Announcement Speech. 2007/02/10 2007. Available: http://www.washingtonpost.com/wp-dyn/content/article/2007/02/10/AR2007021000879.html. 9/12/2009 2009.

List of Barack Obama Presidential Campaign Endorsements, 2008. 2008. Available: http://en.wikipedia.org/wiki/List_of_Barack_Obama_presidential. 8/22/2009 2009.

Media Bias 101: What Journalists Really Think — and What the Public Thinks About the Media. 2010. Available: http://www.mrc.org/static/biasbasics/mediabias101.aspx 2010.

Obama Rally in St. Louis Draws 100,000. 2008/10/18 2008. Available: http://www.huffingtonpost.com/2008/10/18/obama-rally-in-st-louis-d_n_135826.html. 2/4/2010 2010.

Obama Speech Stage Resembles Ancient Greek Temple. 2008. Available: http:\www.reuters.com/articlePrint?articleID=USN2636979020080826. 9/12/2009 2009.

Remarks of Senator Barack Obama: Tbhe American Promise (Democratic Convention). 2008/08/28 2008. Available: http://www.barackobama.com/2008/08/28/remarks_of_senator_barack_obam_108.php.

Sen. Barack Obama (D-Il) Press Conference Manchester, Nh December 10, 2006. 2006/12/10 2006. Available: http://www.gwu.edu/~action/2008/obama/obama121006tr.html. 8/17/2009 2009.

The Confidence of Barack Obama. 2008. Available: http://punditfight.blogspot.com/2008/11/confidence-of-barack-obama-and-part-2.html. 2/2/2010 2010.

The Obama Playbook: How Digital Marketing & Social Media Won the Election: MarketingProfs, LLC, 2009.

Aaker, David A. Building Strong Brands. . New York: The Free Press, 1996.

Abraham, Jay. Getting Everything You Can Out of All You've Got. . New York: Truman Tally Books, 2000.

Bhargava, Rohit. Personality Not Included: Why Companies Lose Their Authenticity - and How Great Brands Get It Back. . New York: McGraw-Hill, 2008.

Blanda, Sean. How to Design Like Barack Obama: Control, Consistency and Change. 2008. Available: http://seanblanda.com/blog/design 2010.

Blumenthal, Howard J. Branded for Life. . Cincinnati, OH: Emmis Books, 2005.

Bonnet, James. Stealing Fire From the Gods: the Complete Guide to Story for Writers and Filmmakers. . Studio City, CA: Michael Wiese Productions, 2006.

Burnett, Bob. Obama's Victory: Three Key Endorsements. 2008/06/12 2008. Available: http://www.huffingtonpost.com/bob-burnett/obamas-victory-three-key_b_106682.html 2010.

Campbell, Joseph. The Hero With a Thousand Faces. . New York: Pantheon Books, 1949.

Caples, John, and Fred E. Hahn. Tested Advertising Methods. . 5th ed. Paramus, NJ: Prentice-Hall, 1997.

Cialdini, Robert B. Influence: the New Psychology of Modern Persuasion. . New York: Quill, 1984.

Coulter, Robin Higie, and Gerald Zaltman. "Using the Zaltman Metaphor Elidtation Technique to Understand Brand Images." Advances in Consumer Research 21 (1994): 501.

Dahl, Melissa. Youth Vote May Have Been Key in Obama's Win. 2008/11/05 2008. Available: http://www.msnbc.com/id/27525497. 8/17/2009 2009.

Davis, Scott M., and Michael Dunn. Building the Brand-Driven Business: Operationalize Your Brand to Drive Profitable Growth. . San Francisco: John Wiley & Sons Inc., 2002.

Dougherty, Steve. Hopes and Dreams: the Story of Barack Obama. . New York: Tess Press, 2008.

Drehle, David Von. Obama's Youth Vote Triumph. 2008/01/04 2008. Available: http://www.time.com/time/politics/article/0,8599,1700525,00.html. 8/17/2009 2009.

Earls, Mark. Herd: How to Change Mass Behavior By Harnessing Our True Nature. . West Sussex: John Wiley & Sons Ltd, 2007.

Feig, Barry. Marketing Straight to the Heart. . New York: AMACOM, a division of American Management Association, 1997.

Festinger, L. A Theory of Cognitive Dissonance. . Stanford, CT: Stanford University Press, 1957.

forman, janis. "When Stories Create an Organization's Future." Strategy & Business Thursday/1 Apr. 1999: 1-4.

Funk, Tom. Web 2.0 and Beyond: Understanding the New Online Business Models, Trends, and Technologies. . Westport, CT: Praeger Publishers, 2009.

Gitomer, Jeffrey H. The Sales Bible: The Ultimate Sales Resource. . New York: Williamr Morrow and Company, Inc., 1994.

Gobe, Marc. Brandjam: Humanizing Brands Through Emotional Design. . New York: Allworth Press, 2007.

Godin, Seth. All Marketers Are Liars: the Power of Telling Authentic Stories in a Low-Trust World. . New York: Portfolio, 2005.

Goldberg, Bernard. A Slobbering Love Affair: the True (And Pathetic) Story of the Torrid Romance Between Barack Obama and the Mainstream Media. . Washington DC: Regnery Publishing, Inc., 2009.

Goldstein, Noah J., Steve J. Martin, and Robert B. Cialdini. Yes!: 50 Scientifically Proven Ways to Be Persuasive. . New York: Free Press, 2008.

Hall, Emma. "If Obama Hadn't Won; a Pepsi Logo for a Maverick Generation." Advertising Age Monday/2 Feb. 2009: 30-30.

Hallward, John. Gimme! the Human Nature of Successful Marketing. . Hoboken, NJ: John Wiley & Sons Inc., 2007.

Hanlon, Patrick. Primal Branding: Create Zealors for Your Brand, Your Company, and Your Future. . New York: Free Press, 2006.

Harfoush, Rahaf. Yes We Did: an Inside Look at How Social Media Built the Obama Brand. . Berkeley, Calif.: New Riders, 2009.

Hass, Christopher. 30 Minute Program: American Stories, American Solutions. 2008/10/29 2008. Available: http://my.barackobama.com/page/community/post/stateu pdates/gGgklx. 2/4/2010 2010.

Hastings, Gerard, Martine Stead, and John Webb. "Fear Appeals in Social Marketing: Strategic and Ethical Reasons for Concern." Psychology and Marketing 21.11 (2004): 961-986.

Haven, Hendall. Storyproof: the Science Behind the Startling Power of Story. . Westport, CT: Libraries Unlimted, 2007.

Hill, Dan. Body of Truth: Leveraging What Consumers Can't Or Won't Say. . Hoboken, NJ: John Wiley & Sons Inc., 2003.

Hogan, Kevin. The Science of Influence: How to Get Anyone to Say Yes in 8 Minutes Or Less! . Hoboken, NJ: John Wiley & Sons Inc., 2005.

Holt, Douglas B. How Brands Become Icons: the Principles of Cultural Branding. . Boston, MA: Harvard Business School Press, 2004.

Hopkins, Claude. Scientific Advertising. . New York: McGraw-Hill/Contemporary, 1966.

Kawasaki, Guy. Creating Customer Evangelists: How Loyal Customers Become a Volunteer Sales Force. . New York, NY: Kaplan Publishing, 2007.

—-Reality Check: the Irreverent Guide to Outsmarting, Outmanaging, and Outmarketing Your Competition. . New York: Penguin Group, Inc., 2008.

Kazmierczak, Elzbieta T. "Design As Meaning Making: From Making Things to the Design of Thinking." Design Issues 19.2 (2003): 45-59.

Kennedy, Dan S. The Ultimate Sales Letter. . 3rd ed. Avon, MA: Adams Media, 2006.

Krippendorff, Kaihan. Barack Obama Is Tapping Into Your Brain. 2009. FastCompany. Available: http://www.fastcompany.com/blog/kaihan-krippendorff. 2/4/2010 2010.

Kushner, Eve. Barack Obama: an Outsider Sets His Sights on the Innermost Circle. 2007. Available: http://www.evekushner.com/writing/?p=167. 8/14/2009 2009.

Leanne, Shel. Say It Like Obama: The Power of Speaking With Purpose and Vision. . New York: McGraw-Hill, 2009.

Loehr, Jim. The Power of Story: Rewrite Your Destiny in Business and in Life. . New York: Free Press, 2007.

Mark, Margaret, and Carol S. Pearson. The Hero and the Outlaw: Building Extraordinary Brands Through the Power of Archetypes. . New York: McGraw-Hill, 2001.

Martin, Neale. Habit: the 95% of Behavior Marketers Ignore. . Upper Saddle River, N.J.: FT Press, 2008.

Mathews, Ryan, and Watts Wacker. What's Your Story? Storytelling to Move Markets, Audiences, People, and Brands. . Upper Saddle River, N.J.: FT Press, 2008.

Maxwell, Richard, and Robert Dickman. The Elements of Persuasion: Use Storytelling to Pitch Better, Sell Faster & Win More Business. . New York: Harper Collins, 2007.

Medina, Hildy. Firms Grab Attention With Unusual Names. 1998. Available: http://www.allbusiness.com/north-america/united-states-california-metro-areas/701003-1.html 2010.

Mendell, David. Obama: From Promise to Power. . New York: Amistad, 2007.

Miller, Robert B., Gary A. Williams, and Alden M. Hayashi. The 5 Paths to Persuasion: the Art of Selling Your Message. . New York: Warner Business Books, 2004.

Neimark, Neil F. The Fight Or Fllight Response. 2010. Available: http://www.thebodysoulconnection.com/EducationCenter/fight.html.

Obama, Barack. Dreams From My Father: a Story of Race and Inheritance. . Revised ed. New York: Three Rivers Press, 2004.

—-The Audacity of Hope: Thoughts on Reclaiming the American Dream. . New York: Three Rivers Press, 2006.

O'Shaughnessy, John, and Nicholas Jackson O'Shaughnessy. The Marketing Power of Emotion. . New York: Oxford University Press, 2003.

Pearson, Carol S. Awakening the Heroes Within: Twelve Archetypes to Help Us Find Ourselves and Transform Our World. . San Francisco: HarperSanFrancisco, 1991.

Plouffe, David. The Audacity to Win: the Inside Story and Lessons of Barack Obama's Historic Victory. . New York, NY: Viking, 2009.

Polyorat, Kawpong, Dana L. Alden, and Eugene S. Kim. "Impact of Narrative Versusfactual Print Ad Copy Onproduct Evaluation: Themediating Role of Admessage Involvement." Psychology & Marketing 24.6 (2007): 539-554.

Rapaille, Clotaire. The Culture Code: An Ingenious Way to Understand Why People Around the World Live and Buy As They Do. . New York: Broadway Books, 2006.

Ries, Al, and Trout. Positioning: the Battle for Your Mind. . 3rd ed. New York: McGraw-Hill, 2000.

Romano, Andrew. Expertinent: Why the Obama "Brand" Is Working. 2008/02/27 2008. Available: http://blog.newsweek.com/blogs/stumper/archive/2008/02/27/how-obama-s-branding-is-working-on-you.aspx 2010.

Rook, Dennis W. "Ritual Dimension of Consumer Behavior." Journal OF Consumer Research 12 (1995): 251.

Ruben Navarrette, Jr. Commentary: Barack Obama, Icy Cool Under Fire. 2008. Available: http://www.cnn.com/2008/POLITICS/10/17/navarrette.debate/index.html. 2/4/2010 2010.

Schmidt, Victoria. 45 Master Characters: Mythic Models for Creating Original Characters. . Cincinnati, OH: Writer's Digest Books, 2007.

Schultz, Don E., and Heidi F. Schultz. Brand Babble: Sense and Nonsense About Branding. . Mason, OH: South-Western Educational Publishing, 2004.

Schwartz, Eugene M. Breakthrough Advertising. . Stamford, CT: Bottom Line Books, 2004. 3rd.

Sherman, Ruth. Get Them to See It Your Way, Right Away: How to Persuade Anyone of Anything. . New York: McGraw-Hill, 2004.

Simmons, Annette. The Story Factor: Inspiration, Influence, and Persuasion Through the Art of Storytelling. . Revised ed. Cambridge, MA: Basic Books, 2006.

Smith, Brian D. "Maybe I Will, Maybe I Won't: What the Connected Perspectives of Motivation Theory and Organisational Commitment May Contribute to Our Understanding of Strategy Implementation." Journal of Strategic Marketing 17.6 (2009): 473-485.

Spiegelman, Eric. Barack Obama's Amazingly Consisten Smile. 2009/09/25 2009. Available: http://www.doobybrain.com/2009/09/25/barack-oba-mas-consistent-smile/ 2010.

Srivastava, Rajendra, and Greg Metz Thomas. The Executive's Guide to Branding: Corporate Performance and Brands - the Risk and Return Effects of Branding, 2005.

State, United StatesDepartmentof, ed. President Barack Obama in His Own Words. . Washington DC: United States Department of State / Bureau of International Information Programs, 2009.

Stelter, Brian. The Facebooker Who Friended Obama. 2008/07/07 2008. Available: http://www.nytimes.com/2008/07/07/technology/07hughes.html 2010.

Stielstra, Greg. Pyro Marketing. . New York: Harper Collins, 2005.

Sutherland, Max, and Alice K. Sylvester. Advertising and the Mind of the Consumer. . St. Leonards Australia: Allen & Unwin, 2000.

Vincent, Laurence. Legendary Brands: Unleashing the Power of Storytelling to Create a Winning Market Strategy. . Chicago, IL: Dearborn Trade Publishing, 2002.

Vitale, Joe. The Attractor Factor. . Hoboken, NJ: John Wiley & Sons, 2005.

Vogler, Christopher. The Writer's Journey: Mythic Structure for Writers. . 2nd ed. Studio City, CA: Michael Wiese Productions, 1998.

Wallis, David. "The Body Politic." Brandweek Monday/31 Mar. 2008: 22-24.

Weeks, Linton. Did Obama Kill Public Campaign Finance? 2008/10/22 2008. Available: http://www.npr.org/templates/story/story.php?/storyId=95957148. 8/14/2009 2009.

Weissman, Jerry. Presenting to Win: the Art of Telling Your Story. . Upper Saddle River, N.J.: FT Prentice Hall Financial Times, 2003.

Wolffe, Richard. Renegade: the Making of a President. . New York: Crown Publishers, 2009.

Zaltman, Gerald, and Robin Highie. "Seeing the Voice of the Customer: Metaphor-Based Advertising Research." Journal of Advertising Research (1995): 35-51.

Zaltman, Gerald. How Customers Think: Essential Insights Into the Mind of the Market. . Boston, MA: Harvard Business School Press, 2003.

Notes:

Chapter 1
1. (Remarks of Senator Barack Obama: Tbhe American
   Promise (Democratic Convention))

Chapter 2
2. (Excerpts From an Interview With Barack Obama)
3. (Martin, N.)
4. (Dougherty, S. 134)
5. (Dougherty, S.)
6. Schultz provides a good primer on traditional branding.
   (Schultz, D. E. and Schultz, H. F.)
7. Zyman offers a good discussion of branding from a mind-
   share perspective. (Srivastava, R. and Thomas, G. M.)
8. *U.S. Election Will Cost $5.3 Billion, Center for Respon-*
   *sive Politics Predicts*2008, 2010/02/01. Retrieved
   2/4/2010, 2010, from
   http://www.opensecrets.org/news/2008/10/us-election-
   will-cost-53-billi.html.
9. Habitual branding can be especially powerful if you tie
   your brand experience into an existing long-term memory of your consumer. This is accomplished through a
   great deal of repetition. (Martin, N. 37)
10. (Weeks, L.)
11. See (Ries, A. and Trout) for a thorough discussion.
12. (Holt, D. B.)
13. The author argues that brands need to shift from com-
    modities to emotion and inspiration in order to become
    more successful. (Gobe, M.)
14. (Aaker)
15. (Dougherty, S.)
16. (Mendell, D.)

17. In this work, the author shows that in order to attract passionate consumers, powerful brands must evoke a dynamic personality.(Bhargava, R.)
18. In his book Dougherty discusses several instances of Obama being booked for rallies versus rock groups themselves, because he was able to sell more tickets(Dougherty, S. 9)
19. Fear appeals to have resonance, but this article cautions that the use of them in the real world may not be as powerful as thought. (Hastings, G., Stead, M. and Webb, J.)
20. (Martin, N. 160)
21. (Holt, D. B. 122)
22. See (Obama, B.) for examples of Obama finding his voice.
23. (Hallward, J. 139)
24. (Feig, B. 151)
25. (Feig, B. 145)
26. (O'Shaughnessy, J. and O'Shaughnessy, N. J. 112)
27. (Harfoush, R.)
28. Holt also argues that brands are helping people fulfill personal stories, which they find themselves living.(Holt, D. B. 36)
29. The younger voter believed that everybody had a role to play and were naturally inclined to be unified. This mindset made them very receptive to Obama's messages of inclusion, unity, and change. (Dahl, M.)
30. This article shows that the under 25-year olds voted for Obama at a rate of 4-1 over his nearest competitors in the Iowa caucuses. It was this vote that was credited for propelling him to victory over Hillary Clinton and giving him the credibility and momentum he needed for the rest of the primary. (Drehle, D. V.)
31. An estimated 22 to 24 million people under age 25 voted in the general election, favoring Obama by wide margins. (Dahl, M.)
32. (Vincent, L.)

33. (Feig, B. 23)
34. (Kawasaki, G. 162)

Chapter 5
35. (Obama, B. 105)
36. (<u>The Confidence of Barack Obama</u>)
37. (<u>The Confidence of Barack Obama</u>)
38. (Plouffe, D.)
39. (Smith, B. D.)
40. (Vitale, J.)
41. (Abraham, J.)
42. (Gitomer, J. H.)

Chapter 7
43. (Obama, B. 155)
44. Decision-making requires the use of both logic and emotion. In fact, it could be argued that the emotional complement comes first and therefore has more resonance than logic.(Zaltman, G. 8)
45. Martin points out that people make decisions with executive (i.e., rational) and habitual (i.e., emotional) minds. The executive mind causes people to consciously focus on one thing at a time whereas the habitual mind allows us to bypass this mental energy relying upon previously learned heuristics. (Martin, N. 15)
46. (Obama, B. 158)
47. (Hill, D.)
48. Zaltman introduces his technique for eliciting metaphors in this work. (Zaltman, G. and Highie, R.)
49. Iconic brands actually lead culture rather than following culture. This is accomplished by taking a provocative stand against the status quo, which is being seen as the contradiction of ideologies. In fact Holt would argue that a true iconic brand will not really become iconic unless and until it alienates people who hold contradicting viewpoints. This is imperative to understand especially in the realm of politics, where it is true that powerful enemies make for better fans.(Holt, D. B. 122)

50. (<u>Barack Obama - Words That Inspired a Nation</u>)
51. When Obama entered the Democratic Primary race, 37% of the nation's public did not even know who he was. Among likely Democratic voters, less than 10% thought of him as a viable candidate. (Dougherty, S. 134)
52. Obama successfully raised more than $575 million over the course of his campaign. In the final months of the general election, Obama raised $428 million to McCain's $190 million. In addition, McCain had accepted federal funding thus limiting his spending to $84 million. (Weeks, L.)
53. Focusing on the habitual mind has four powerful implications: 1) Marketing organizations need to focus on behavior, not attitudes or beliefs; 2) The habitual mind learns through cause and effect, not reason; 3)In order to hold onto consumers, you don't want them to consciously think about you; 4) In order to get customers away from competitors, you must get them to consciously think about you. These ideas can be very powerful when trying to gain market share as a new entrant. When Barack Obama came up against Hillary Clinton in the primaries, one of his first tasks was to take the established Democratic voter and get him/her to consider and ultimately switch to Obama. (Martin, N. 16)
54. Martin argues that customers are loyal to trusted brands so that they don't have to think about their purchases with a new and competing brand. If you can show a violation of trust from the entrenched brand then your brand could have a chance of getting into the mindset of the consumer. (Martin, N. 131)
55. (Dougherty, S.)
56. (Dougherty, S.)
57. (<u>Barack Obama - Words That Inspired a Nation</u>)
58. (Martin, N. 160)
59. (Feig, B.)
60. (Dougherty, S.)

61. (Dahl, M.)
62. (Drehle, D. V.)
63. (Leanne, S.)
64. Our current culture suggests that a majority of our culturally transmitted ideas come from our peers and not our history. This is especially prevalent in times of rapid change and technology advances. The result of this is that people often face uncertainty in their day-to-day life, especially with rapid change. When faced with fundamental uncertainties we tend to rely upon culturally transmitted myths to understand and live our lives. (Zaltman, G. 227)
65. (Obama, B.)
66. (Kushner, E.)
67. In order to attract passionate consumers powerful brands must evoke a dynamic personality.(Bhargava, R.)
68. Fear appeals to have resonance, but this article cautions that the use of them in the real world may not be as powerful as thought. (Hastings, G., Stead, M. and Webb, J.)
69. Goldstein shows that simple words and ideas lead to people feeling more positive about the brand. While Barack Obama's name was not familiar to most, the word "change" allowed people to interpret his ideas more easily and therefore associate positive feelings to his campaign. (Goldstein, N. J., Martin, S. J. and Cialdini, R. B. 159)
70. (Dougherty, S.)
71. "The problem of gangs was too general to make an impression on people - issues had to be made concrete, specific, and winnable." (Obama, B. 162)

Chapter 9
72. (Krippendorff, K.)
73. (Haven, H. 3)
74. (Maxwell, R. and Dickman, R.)
75. (Vogler, C. 1)

76. (Campbell)
77. (Leanne, S.)
78. (Obama, B.)
79. (Obama, B.)
80. (Mathews, R. and Wacker, W. 29)
81. (Godin, S. 14)
82. (Zaltman, G. 228)
83. (Wolffe, R. 86)
84. (Wolffe, R. 63)
85. (Mendell, D. 155)
86. (Hill, D. 156)
87. (Vincent, L.)
88. (Bonnet, J. 166)
89. (Maxwell, R. and Dickman, R.)
90. (Godin, S. 41)
91. One merely needs to search on the topic of Barack Obama and pandering to see that many have (and continue to) accused him of pandering to core constituencies. For one example see (<u>Dobbs Asked If Obama Is "Pandering to Ethnocentric Special Interests Again" By Accepting Richardson's Endorsement</u>)
92. (Hanlon, P.)
93. (Wolffe, R. 65)
94. (Loehr, J.)
95. It can be shown that stories told during business settings are very effective at conveying business culture. See ("Once Upon a Time: When a Meeting Of the Minds Isn't Enough, try a Meeting of The emotions: Tell a Story..")
96. ("Once Upon a Time: When a Meeting Of the Minds Isn't Enough, try a Meeting of The emotions: Tell a Story..")
97. (Bhargava, R. 101)
98. (forman 3)
99. (Dougherty, S.)
100. (Hill, D. 143)
101. (Polyorat, K., Alden, D. L. and Kim, E. S. 548)

102. (Hass, C.)
103. (Mathews, R. and Wacker, W. 12)

Chapter 10
104. (Barack Obama Quotes)
105. (Vogler, C.)
106. (Pearson)
107. (Schmidt, V.)
108. For a good discussion on twelve classic archetypes that we encounter in business, see (Mark and Pearson)
109. (Mark and Pearson)
110. For a thorough and entertaining discussion of how most consumers follow the herd, see (Earls, M.)
111. (Dougherty, S.)
112. (Wolffe, R. 197)
113. For just one of many commentaries about Obama's "coolness", refer to (Ruben Navarrette, J.). This commentary came late in the general election campaign and shows how Obama's cool was swaying many pundits and voters.
114. (Dougherty, S.)
115. (Fainting Rallies)
116. (Kennedy, D. S.)
117. (Feig, B. 151)
118. (Wolffe, R. 55)
119. (Obama, B. 11)
120. (Kushner, E.)
121. (Hallward, J. 139)
122. (Medina, H.)
123. (Hopkins)
124. (Obama, B.)
125. (Bhargava, R.)
126. (Obama, B.)
127. (Obama, B. 6)
128. (Obama, B. 356)
129. (Kennedy, D. S.)
130. (Kawasaki, G.)

Chapter 11
131. (Simmons, A.)
132. (Neimark)
133. (Holt, D. B. 36)
134. (O'Shaughnessy, J. and O'Shaughnessy, N. J. 42)
135. (Obama, B.)
136. (Holt, D. B.)
137. (Festinger)
138. (O'Shaughnessy, J. and O'Shaughnessy, N. J. 37)
139. (Holt, D. B. 122)
140. (Wolffe, R. 43)
141. (Obama, B.)
142. (Dougherty, S.)
143. (Martin, N. 131)
144. (<u>Barack Obama - Words That Inspired a Nation</u>)
145. (Dahl, M.)
146. (Zaltman, G. 227)
147. (Dougherty, S.)
148. (Godin, S. 133)

Chapter 13
149. (<u>Barack Obama - Words That Inspired a Nation</u>)
150. (Coulter, R. H. and Zaltman, G.)
151. (Bonnet, J. 37)
152. (Gobe, M.)
153. (Aaker)
154. (Mendell, D. 39)
155. (Obama, B. 92)
156. (Bonnet, J. 37)
157. (<u>Illinois Sen. Barack Obama's Announcement Speech</u>)
158. (<u>Obama Speech Stage Resembles Ancient Greek Temple</u>)
159. (Wolffe, R. 84)
160. (Zaltman, G. 228...)
161. (Zaltman, G.)
162. (Martin, N. 15)
163. (Hill, D.)

164. (Zaltman, G.)
165. (Goldstein, N. J., Martin, S. J. and Cialdini, R. B. 159)
166. (Rapaille, C.)
167. It was widely reported that Obama campaign rallies would typically draw thousands of people. For one of his last rallies before the general election, he drew an estimated 100,000 people, the largest crowd ever reported (<u>Obama Rally in St. Louis Draws 100,000</u>)
168. When emotions are combined with trust, you get a great deal of loyalty from your audience. (O'Shaughnessy, J. and O'Shaughnessy, N. J. 4)
169. (O'Shaughnessy, J. and O'Shaughnessy, N. J. 79)
170. (Feig, B. 23)
171. (O'Shaughnessy, J. and O'Shaughnessy, N. J. 87)
172. (Mathews, R. and Wacker, W. 28)

Chapter 14
173. (<u>Sen. Barack Obama (D-Il) Press Conference Manchester, Nh December 10, 2006</u>)
174. Claude Hopkins is thought to be the originator of most modern advertising principles. His original work, published in 1923, can be found in the public domain. (Hopkins)
175. (Schwartz, E. M.)
176. (Hallward, J. 140)
177. (Sherman, R.)
178. (<u>Barack Obama - Words That Inspired a Nation</u>)
179. (Weissman, J. 9)
180. (Feig, B. 162)
181. When studying two consumer products, narrative ads were shown to be more appealing than factual ads as well as causing higher levels of message involvement for the consumer. (Polyorat, K., Alden, D. L. and Kim, E. S. 548)
182. (Gitomer, J. H.)
183. (Obama, B.)
184. (Kennedy, D. S.)

185. (Caples, J. and Hahn, F. E. 30)
186. Barack Obama mastered the art of asking rhetorical questions and telling stories in his speeches and ads. Nearly all of his speeches used one or more of these devices to gain attention. (<u>Barack Obama - Words That Inspired a Nation</u>)
187. (Drehle, D. V.)
188. This book discusses how the majority of people can be classified as "followers" in their persuasion. These people make decisions based on how other trusted people have made them in the past. Once you can get enough people on board initially, these people will join the bandwagon. (Miller, R. B., Williams, G. A. and Hayashi, A. M. 9)
189. (Godin, S.)
190. (Obama, B. 162)
191. (Dougherty, S.)
192. (<u>Barack Obama - Words That Inspired a Nation</u>)
193. (<u>Barack Obama - Words That Inspired a Nation</u>)
194. (O'Shaughnessy, J. and O'Shaughnessy, N. J. 21)
195. (O'Shaughnessy, J. and O'Shaughnessy, N. J. 50)
196. (O'Shaughnessy, J. and O'Shaughnessy, N. J. 87)
197. (<u>Barack Obama - Words That Inspired a Nation</u>)
198. (<u>List of Barack Obama Presidential Campaign Endorsements, 2008</u>)
199. This book discusses how the majority of people can be classified as "followers" in their persuasion. These people make decisions based on how other trusted people have made them in the past. Once you can get enough people on board initially, these people will join the bandwagon. (Miller, R. B., Williams, G. A. and Hayashi, A. M. 9)
200. People can often be made to conform to the viewpoints of others. Effective advertising will reinforce the message making conformity more likley to occur. (Sutherland, M. and Sylvester, A. K. 44)

201. For more evidence of conformity and how people change beliefs based on peer pressure, read (Blumenthal, H. J. 35)
202. (O'Shaughnessy, J. and O'Shaughnessy, N. J. 26)
203. (O'Shaughnessy, J. and O'Shaughnessy, N. J. 39)

Chapter 16
204. (State, U. S. 89)
205. (Hanlon, P.)
206. (Hanlon, P.)
207. (Martin, N. 16)
208. (O'Shaughnessy, J. and O'Shaughnessy, N. J.)
209. (Davis, S. M. and Dunn, M.)
210. ("Hit Or Miss: How Will 2008 Be Remembered in Marketing Circles?.")
211. (Mathews, R. and Wacker, W.)
212. (Leanne, S.)
213. (Wallis, D.)
214. ("The Rise and Fall of Brand Hillary.")
215. (Wolffe, R. 48)
216. (The Obama Playbook: How Digital Marketing & Social Media Won the Election)
217. (Plouffe, D.)
218. (Weeks, L.)
219. ("Hit Or Miss: How Will 2008 Be Remembered in Marketing Circles?.")
220. (Hall, E.)
221. (Romano, A.)
222. (Kazmierczak, E. T.)
223. (Romano, A.)
224. (Blanda, S.)
225. (Blanda, S.)
226. (Blanda, S.)
227. (About Organizing for America)
228. (Ruben Navarrette, J.)
229. (Spiegelman, E.)

Chapter 18

230. (Miller, R. B., Williams, G. A. and Hayashi, A. M. 9)
231. (Burnett, B.)
232. (Plouffe, D.)
233. (Harfoush, R.)
234. (Stelter, B.)
235. (Mendell, D. 10)
236. (Goldberg, B.)
237. (Media Bias 101: What Journalists Really Think — and What the Public Thinks About the Media)
238. (Stielstra, G. 100)
239. (Plouffe, D.)
240. (Wolffe, R. 81)
241. (Cialdini)
242. (Stielstra, G. 124)
243. (Hogan, K. 91)
244. (Stielstra, G. 119)
245. (Harfoush, R.)
246. (Stielstra, G. 6)
247. (The Obama Playbook: How Digital Marketing & Social Media Won the Election)
248. (The Obama Playbook: How Digital Marketing & Social Media Won the Election)
249. (Funk, T.)
250. (Funk, T.)
251. (Harfoush, R.)
252. (Plouffe, D.)
253. (Rook, D. W.)
254. (Harfoush, R.)
255. (Harfoush, R.)

Breinigsville, PA USA
28 July 2010
242618BV00004B/1/P